DATE DUE

APR 1 0 1995	
APR 2 6 1995	
MAY - 8 1995	
FEB 1 6 1996	
MAR 2 1 1996	
APR 0 3 1996	
APR 0 4 1996	
APR 2 5 1996	
JUL 29 1996	
AUG 1 5 1996	
B958058	
AUG 1 5 1996	
MAR 3 1 1999	

BRODART	Cat. No. 23-221

MASS COMMUNICATION AND PUBLIC HEALTH

OTHER RECENT VOLUMES IN THE
SAGE FOCUS EDITIONS

MASS COMMUNICATION AND PUBLIC HEALTH

Complexities and Conflicts

Charles Atkin
Lawrence Wallack
editors

SAGE PUBLICATIONS
The International Professional Publishers
Newbury Park   London   New Delhi

For information address:

SAGE Publications, Inc.
2111 West Hillcrest Drive
Newbury Park, California 91320

SAGE Publications Ltd.
28 Banner Street
London EC1Y 8QE
England

SAGE Publications India Pvt. Ltd.
M-32 Market
Greater Kailash I
New Delhi 110 048 India

Printed in the United States of America

Library of Congress Cataloging-in-Publication Data

Main entry under title:

Mass communication and public health: complexities and conflicts /
   edited by Charles Atkin and Lawrence Wallack
          p.   cm. — (Sage focus editions ; v. 121)
     Includes bibliographical references and index
     ISBN 0-8039-3924 (c). — ISBN 0-8039-3925-6 (p)
     1. Mass media in health education.   I. Atkin, Charles K.
   II. Wallack, Lawrence Marshall.
   RA440.5.M37   1990
   362.1'014—dc20   90-39610
                                                                 CIP

FIRST PRINTING, 1990

Sage Production Editor: Astrid Virding

Contents

Preface

Alcohol, tobacco, other drugs, poor diet, and lack of exercise are health risk factors contributing to the majority of premature mortality in the United States. Cigarette smoking alone accounts for almost one-quarter of the two million deaths that occur each year. The mass media represent an important vehicle for communicating information about these risk factors to the population on a regular basis.

However, information does not equal prevention, and even the most comprehensive public information campaigns have achieved rather limited success. Furthermore, encouraging individuals to change their behavior is only a partial solution to socially created health problems.

This book evolved from a recent national conference that was convened to explore how the mass media could become a more potent weapon to improve public health. The original premise of the conference organizers was that the information dissemination function is important and should be improved through the development of better campaigns and the integration of informational content into news and entertainment programming. This book will provide much useful material for those seeking to stretch the boundaries of the mass media as a direct health educator.

A more fundamental contribution of this book is the insights it provides into the workings of the media and how this influences the public health agenda. True progress toward enhancing public health involves moving beyond the strategy of providing information to individuals, to promoting the role of environmental factors (e.g., social, economic, and political forces) as determinants of health. While information dissemination about personal risk factors is generally noncontroversial, this is not the case when the focus shifts to public policy issues. For example, the broadcast industry easily embraces the "designated driver" concept for drunk driving prevention, but is antagonistic to limitations on alcoholic beverage advertising or increases in the alcohol excise tax, even though the latter is scientifically demonstrated to be the single most effective means of reducing alcohol-related problems.

The conference that generated this volume convened experts from the fields of journalism, advertising, entertainment, communication science, public policy, medical science, and public health. Participants included practitioners, academic scholars, and representatives from government agencies and advocacy groups. The meeting, held at the Annenberg Center for Health Sciences in Rancho Mirage, California, was primarily sponsored by several federal agencies (Office of Disease Prevention and Health Promotion, Office for Substance Abuse Prevention, and National Cancer Institute).

The conference sought to achieve several goals: increasing understanding of mass communication influences on health issues and problems, exploring shared responsibilities among media and public health professionals, designing strategies for influencing policymakers and gatekeepers in each field, and setting priorities for future initiatives and research.

This book presents edited versions of eight key papers commissioned for the conference (Chapters 2, 3, 4, 5, 6, 7, 8, and 10), along with an overview (Chapter 1), two new contributions (Chapters 9 and 11), and a set of commentaries (Afterword) by conference participants.

Chapter 1, by health communication specialists Charles Atkin and Elaine Bratic Arkin, provides an overview of the complexities and conflicts involving mass media and public health at the beginning of the 1990s, reflecting discussions and presentations from the conference. The authors describe how the evolving relationship between the mass media and public health sectors is played out in the context of a rapidly changing media and regulatory environment, and they identify the conflicting priorities of these two diverse communities. The chapter addresses issues in the four basic domains of advertising, journalism, entertainment, and information campaigns.

In the section on advertising issues, Atkin and Arkin note the emergence of a fundamental trend toward combining public health messages with commercial messages in the form of public/private partnerships and health-related advertising practices. The section on news coverage of health examines journalistic imperatives, media relations for health institutions, and challenges of using news media as vehicles for health education. The overview of entertainment issues focuses on pragmatic advocacy approaches for shaping television programming portrayals of health. The authors summarize key strategies for effective information campaigns. The chapter also features a series of academic research priorities and a set of recommendations for the public health community.

In Chapter 2, public health expert Lawrence Wallack offers a provocative perspective on the role of mass media in health promotion. He notes how the broad reach of mass communication channels and the public's reliance on media messages represent great promise for promoting health. However, Wallack argues that the mass media can be an obstacle to change by reducing health issues to problems of individual behavior, by advertising health-compromising products, and by reinforcing existing arrangements that favor bottom-line considerations over public health concerns.

Philip Meyer, a journalism professor with 20 years of experience as a science writer, presents an overview of the factors that determine news media responsiveness to public health in Chapter 3. He identifies both the traditional and the nontraditional criteria defining news value, and he points out how the coverage of health is shaped by market demand, consensus and competition within the news community, and pressure from advertisers. Meyer advocates an increase in specialized health reporting and more proactive efforts by health professionals to communicate knowledge to the public.

Journalistic imperatives are also examined in Chapter 4 by Stephen Klaidman, former reporter at *The New York Times*. He notes that the recent increase in service-oriented coverage of health matters has helped to overcome basic shortcomings of traditional hard-news treatment of science and health. In discussing news, Klaidman emphasizes two key logics determining coverage: impact on the core middle-class constituency (illustrated by the case of the media underplaying the AIDS story in the early 1980s), and hypothesis-based investigative journalism (with a detailed critique of a flawed exposé of cancer research). He suggests that health news can be improved by increasing the public's health knowledge and by educating reporters and editors about the field of public health.

Stephen Stuyck discusses the response of the public health community to the news media from his perspective as a public affairs officer at a major cancer center (Chapter 5). Noting that there are fundamental conflicts between the fields of public health and journalism, he argues that there is an unequal relationship that poses special problems and challenges for those working in biomedical science, health care institutions, and public health education. Based on his practical experience and a recent survey of media gatekeepers, Stuyck offers suggestions to the public health community for making health information more understandable, compelling, and easily accessible.

Two chapters examine health-related advertising practices and regulations. In Chapter 6, William Novelli draws upon his experience as the head of a major advertising and social marketing firm to describe the role of commercial messages in the mass media. He discusses several controversial issues in the promotion of health-related products, beginning with an examination of various claims in foods advertising. This is followed by a description of problems associated with advertising of three sensitive product categories: alcohol, cigarettes, and pharmaceuticals. Novelli also explores avenues of cooperation between commercial and public health sectors (illustrated by the collaboration between Kellogg's and the National Cancer Institute) and the concept of social responsibility in marketing. Lawyer Bruce Silverglade of the Center for Science in the Public Interest, a Washington-based consumer advocacy group, focuses on public and private regulatory policies affecting communication of public health information (Chapter 7). He traces the stages of progression of policymaking over the past two decades, from control-oriented government regulation to reliance on free-market forces to declining self-regulation. Silverglade cautiously espouses public-private partnerships to promote nutrition education, with food industry participation encouraged by regulatory inducements.

The entertainment media, particularly prime-time television series, portray health themes that reach tens of millions of people each day. This content may contribute to incidental learning by individuals who might not seek out serious health information from conventional sources. Chapters 8 and 9 explore topics relating to television and health.

In the chapter on television images and impact, Nancy Signorielli draws upon her lengthy research experience on the "Cultural Indicators" project at the University of Pennsylvania's Annenberg School of Communication. She reviews content analysis findings and selected

studies of audience effects regarding many key types of health entertainment depictions, including illnesses, doctors, nutrition, smoking,
drinking, sexuality, and AIDS. While there is a substantial body of
research systematically describing TV health portrayals, Signorielli
points out the need to investigate how these images influence the
knowledge, attitudes, and behaviors of the viewing audience.

Kathryn Montgomery of the UCLA Film and Television Department
has conducted a six-year study of the relationship between advocacy
groups and the television entertainment industry. Her chapter focuses
on the process by which "Hollywood lobbyists" attempt to influence
writers and producers to incorporate certain health issues into prime-
time programming. Montgomery describes a number of case studies
where advocacy organizations inside and outside the industry have
shaped the portrayal of alcohol, abortion, AIDS, and other sensitive
topics. The most successful efforts involve cooperative approaches that
sensitize the creative community to key issues and provide helpful
advice and valuable resource materials.

In Chapter 10, health communication researchers Brian Flay and Dee
Burton distill a broad body of theory and evidence pertaining to the
conditions under which mass media health campaigns achieve the
greatest impact on the public. They identify a number of key principles
for successful public health campaigns, including research-based development of influential messages delivered by believable sources, frequent and consistent dissemination through media channels in a manner
that attracts the attention of target audiences, and stimulation of favorable interpersonal communication. They point out the importance of
designing campaigns that will exert influence beyond awareness and
knowledge, particularly changes in individuals' behaviors, through
various hierarchies of effects; stimulation of broader societal change
is also crucial. Summative evaluation of campaign effects is recommended for accumulating valuable knowledge to guide future campaign
strategies.

Lawrence Wallack returns in Chapter 11 to delineate and compare
the social marketing and media advocacy approaches to promoting
health. He argues that social marketing offers a false promise that
individual behavior change will significantly improve health when the
key determinants of health are external to the individual. He concludes
that it will be necessary to rely on the more policy-oriented media
advocacy approach as the primary health promotion strategy, but ac-
knowledges that public communication campaigns based on social

marketing principles play an important role in informing the public about personal risk factors.

The closing "Afterword" section presents implications for mass media and health issues by respected specialists representing government, media industry, advocacy, and academic perspectives. A pragmatic view from the federal government vantage point is provided by Elaine Bratic Arkin (communication consultant to several health agencies), Robert Denniston (head of communication programs for the Office for Substance Abuse Services), and Rose Mary Romano (public information chief at the Office of Smoking and Health), who appraise the barriers and opportunities in the early 1990s. Former CBS Vice President George Dessart assesses the forces reshaping the broadcasting business and the consequences of the new media environment for health communication. Michael Pertschuk, a former Federal Trade Commission Chairman who currently directs the Advocacy Institute, discusses strategies for using the news media to advance public health causes. The fourth perspective is contributed by communication researchers Everett Rogers and Arvind Singhal of the Annenberg School of Communications at the University of Southern California; they report on recent studies examining the combination of entertainment and education in health promotion.

In sum, the book provides a foundation enabling mass media and public health professionals better to understand each other and to work together more effectively. It represents a new starting point for discussing improved use of the media and sets the stage for advancing beyond simple information dissemination to a more basic reordering of the public health agenda and development of healthy public policies.

As indicated earlier, much of the material for this book was presented at the Rancho Mirage conference. The Annenberg Center has produced a 25-minute TV program featuring conference highlights. This production summarizes key conclusions from discussion sessions and includes excerpts from speeches and relevant examples of health-related media content from soap operas, commercials, and public service announcements. The videotape is a useful supplement to this book, especially for college classes. Instructors can obtain a free copy of the tape from the federal clearinghouse, NCADI, P.O. 2345, Rockville, MD 20852.

Finally, the editors would like to express appreciation to several individuals who played a major role in organizing the conference: Elaine Arkin, Robert Denniston, and Rose Mary Romano, along with David McCallum of the Institute for Health Policy Analysis, Georgetown University.

1

Issues and Initiatives in Communicating Health Information to the Public

CHARLES ATKIN
ELAINE BRATIC ARKIN

This introductory chapter provides an overview of the complexities and conflicts involving mass media and public health at the beginning of the 1990s. Much of the material reflects discussions and presentations from a recent national conference, which brought together experts from the fields of journalism, advertising, entertainment, communication science, public policy, medical science, and public health. Participants included practitioners, academic scholars, and representatives from government agencies and advocacy groups.

The conference was designed to increase understanding of the influences of mass communication on health issues and problems, to explore shared responsibilities among media and public health professionals, to design strategies for influencing policymakers and gatekeepers in the mass media and public health fields, and to set priorities for future initiatives and research.

The evolving relationship between the mass communication and public health sectors is played out in the context of a rapidly changing media and regulatory environment. First, there is a trend toward diversification of the media. The three television networks now account for only two-thirds of all television viewing, as exposure to independent stations, cable channels, and VCRs has grown dramatically. The networks must compete more aggressively for advertisers, which may threaten the independence of TV news and entertainment. Second, public interest in health information has increased in recent years; there is a corresponding rise in health-related media content and health claims in advertising, and both advertisers and broadcasters are more sensitive to public opinion and to organized advocacy efforts of special-interest groups. Third, the Reagan administration introduced an era of deregulation, resulting in less public service time for public health messages and less oversight of health-related portrayals and advertising claims by severely trimmed network "standards and practices" departments.

Another major trend is toward greater message competition and clutter, especially on television. There has been a sharp increase in 15 second spots, and large numbers of TV viewers "zap" ads or public service announcements (PSAs) that they find boring or discrepant. With the broad array of alternative cable channels and ease of remote control devices, "grazing" viewers display high rates of switching channels in search of more stimulating entertainment or informational material.

In his address opening the conference, former CBS News President Van Gordon Sauter likened the mass media to a six-tier loom upon which health messages can be woven into a finely crafted fabric: radio (with its directness and immediacy), television (with cinematic revelation), daily newspapers (with detail and background), weekly magazines (with rich context), monthly magazines (with perceptions afforded by widely spaced deadlines), and books (with documentation and perspective).

His comments focused on television and its basic content forms: news, entertainment, commercials, and public service announcements. He referred to research over the past two decades showing that of all the discretionary areas of news, the category of health and wellness is by far the most popular with the viewing audience. TV news organizations have increasingly seized upon health reporting as a means of developing and sustaining the audience, ranging from the proliferation of TV doctors to cooperative projects with local health organizations. According to Sauter, much of this promise is yet unrealized: "In my years of being involved in news at various levels, I have always thought that the health organizations failed to seize upon the potential in television and the way the television news organizations can be exploited for the dissemination of whatever special-interest information might be."

On the entertainment side, he observed that the two great franchises in television are detectives and doctors. Programming about doctors and health have three major advantages to programmers: the life-and-death stakes in any story about doctors and patients, the clear dramatic resolution of the medical problem, and the audience desire to see their health professionals idealized.

Although network television draws the most attention as the prime medium for health messages, it is important to note that the audience share of NBC, ABC, and CBS has declined steadily in recent years. Health educators should look beyond network TV and the other "traditional mainline" media (e.g., major daily newspapers and widely circulated magazines) to consider a broad array of dissemination channels: cable networks, independent TV stations, videotapes, movie theater slides, newsletters, billboards, transit cards, and booklets. Within a basic medium such as television or newspapers, there is also a great variety of potential vehicles beyond the standard PSA or news item, including editorial commentary, letters to the editor, local talk shows, music videos, and paid advertisements. The remarkable diversity of the mass media offers extensive opportunities for reaching the American public.

One of the barriers that health campaigners face is audience sensitivity, particularly for material that media gatekeepers perceive to be potentially offensive to their mass audiences. Networks have turned down certain PSAs that are regarded as too sensitive (e.g., adolescent pregnancy prevention messages advocating contraception, and AIDS spots referring to condoms). The problem also applies to entertainment portrayals of "controversial" subject matter. However, this sensitivity may be more perceived than real, based on a vocal, mobilized minority that exerts a disproportionate amount of influence upon rather timid mass media outlets. The public health community may seek to counter these pressure groups by activating previously silent segments of the public or by objectively measuring overall public opinion, in order to correct the misconceptions of gatekeepers.

The discussions at the conference centered on the conflicts among the functions and goals of the the mass communication and public health sectors, as outlined in the following chart:

Conflicting priorities of mass media versus public health institutions

Mass media objectives	Public health objectives
To entertain, persuade, or inform	To educate
To make a profit	To improve public health
To reflect society	To change society
To address personal concerns	To address societal concerns
To cover short-term events	To conduct long-term campaigns
To deliver salient pieces of material	To create understanding of complex information

These disparate objectives pose many problems both for health educators utilizing mass communication to influence the public and for media professionals dealing with health topics in covering news, creating entertainment, and devising advertisements. This chapter will address a number of issues, controversies, conflicts, opportunities, and initiatives arising in the four basic domains of advertising, journalism, entertainment, and information campaigns.

ADVERTISING ISSUES

The American mass media rest on a commercial foundation upon which marketers and health professionals must operate. In Chapter 6, Novelli observes that commercial communications practitioners in the disciplines of advertising and public relations have been quite successful in utilizing the mass media to achieve corporate goals of sales and profit. Public health specialists are often critical of the influence of these private sector messages, but health promoters might be well advised to borrow certain sophisticated practices from advertisers. In particular, public health educators have yet fully to embrace the well-known social marketing principles described in the second Wallack chapter (Chapter 11). Flay and Burton also recommend that health campaigners should pattern their messages after certain approaches used by commercial persuaders (Chapter 10).

Marketing communication is subject to numerous dynamic shifts and pressures, due to the rapidly evolving nature of media institutions, consumer preferences, and government regulations. The recent environmental changes discussed in the introductory section have important implications for mass media marketers in the health arena.

Emerging from the interplay of these developments is a fundamental trend toward combining public health messages with commercial messages, in the form of private/public partnerships and health-related advertising practices. These new prospects offer the public health community an opportunity for wider dissemination of information but raise questions of accuracy, compromise, and control. For the media and marketing communities, the changes promise consumer appeal and co-sponsorship by credible nonprofit sources but pose questions of social responsibility and self-regulation. As a result, there is increased debate about the need to serve the public interest in determining which products should be marketed via the mass media and in setting guidelines for appropriate advertising practices. These are among the issues examined by Novelli and Silverglade (Chapters 6 and 7); this overview will focus on the partnership and advertising practices topics.

Growth of Private/Public Partnerships

In the mid-1980s, the Kellogg Corporation and the National Cancer Institute (NCI) collaborated in producing advertisements that simultaneously promoted a Kellogg cereal and NCI's fiber message. This successful partnership has prompted many companies and trade associations to pursue cooperative ventures with NCI and other public health agencies and organizations.

For public health communicators, collaboration with commercial marketers has pragmatic advantages. The private resources enable messages to be packaged more effectively and disseminated more widely; ad placement in prime-time slots is particularly attractive in an era when public service access is diminishing. From the private sector's perspective, collaboration is advantageous because it helps fulfill a social responsibility while accomplishing marketing goals because public sector endorsement increases the credibility of their products.

However, a number of problematic issues arise. There is a basic incompatibility between the complexities and uncertainties of medical science versus the need to convey simple health messages in advertisements. For example, fiber is not a certain good; there are numerous kinds of fiber, many of which scientists cannot yet differentiate, and some of which may actually contribute to development of cancer.

Second, there is potential for misleading messages. While the NCI/Kellogg collaboration is considered a model of responsible health marketing, there are concerns that other companies might manipulate scientific information in an irresponsible manner. There is a need to develop appropriate guidelines for advertisers to ensure that claims are accurate and truthful. However, promulgation of elaborate rules may stifle activity and require complex enforcement mechanisms. Pursuing a combination of informal guidelines and quiet negotiation (backed by the prospect of counteradvertising or negative publicity) may be more productive than resorting to formal regulation or litigation.

A third issue concerns the process of forming and implementing partnership arrangements. Health agencies seek to exercise close control, which may raise transaction costs for corporations to an unacceptable level. There must be mutual benefit for collaboration to work, requiring flexibility and compromise to consummate such relationships. However, public health specialists are concerned that cooperation may lead to cooptation. It should also be recognized that the participation of private organizations may require pragmatic inducements or pressures from government regulatory agencies.

Growth of Controversial Advertising Practices

Since the 1970s, there has been a decline in government regulation and monitoring of advertising, and a number of advertising practices have drawn criticism because of potentially detrimental health implications. A central issue in recent years involves alcohol and cigarette advertisements targeted at vulnerable audiences, such as heavy drinkers, youth, or minorities. Another sensitive product category is prescription medicine; pharmaceutical firms are increasingly turning to direct-to-consumer advertising, which is regarded with concern by government agencies and health organizations.

The claims and images presented in advertisements for a wide variety of products have also generated controversy. Beyond outright inaccuracies, there are problems associated with omission of essential information (e.g., ads promoting canned soup as healthful without disclosing the high amount of sodium, or ads for risky products that do not provide warnings about improper use). Imagery that links a questionable product to a healthy lifestyle may be misleading, even if specific claims are not advanced. In lieu of federal regulation, advertisers have a responsibility to develop self-regulatory codes to prevent these problems. Since individual companies hesitate to adopt unilateral restrictions, industry-wide trade associations are in a better position to implement code provisions.

Government policies can play an important role in shaping the practices of advertisers. Control-oriented regulations of federal agencies in the 1970s ultimately foundered due to the lack of a forceful constituency during the ensuing era of deregulation. Laissez-faire approaches resulted in an upswing in misleading and deceptive health claims, especially in the advertising of food products. Historically, the most stringent regulatory approach has been applied to cigarettes: the FTC required that ads disclose tar and nicotine content, broadcasters were required to run antismoking countermessages, TV and radio advertising was finally banned, and warning labels were required on packages and print ads. The current battleground has shifted to alcohol advertising, with a wide variety of policy options under debate.

Based on the current alcohol advertising research showing relatively modest degrees of harmful effects and the pragmatic political barriers to fundamental change, imposition of broad-scale ban on advertising does not appear to be warranted or feasible. A more promising approach is to pursue a combination of government and industry initiatives designed to eliminate a limited array of the most problematic advertising practices, to increase the quantity and prominence of prohealth and safety countermessages, to insert additional disclaimers and positive role modeling in ads, and to improve the legitimate educational quality of brand-sponsored public service ads that promote moderation or warn against drunk driving. This will require a more enlightened (and less self-serving) implementation of the social responsibility concept on the part of the advertising, media, and alcohol industries, and a more assertive role for government agencies and advocacy organizations in facilitating reform. Innovative arrangements for collaborative efforts between representatives of the private and public sectors might be explored as a fruitful alternative to the standard confrontational stances in addressing alcohol advertising issues.

Finally, there is a need to educate consumers to evaluate more critically the advertising that they encounter. Schools are introducing units to teach students techniques for interpreting TV commercials, but little consumer education has been provided to the general public. Specifically, people need to know how to weigh conflicting claims and understand the meaning of certain health advantages that are featured in advertisements. The development of a simplified grading system quantifying the degree of benefits and risks would help consumers in sorting through the confusing welter of health information (and misinformation) bombarding them from marketers.

NEWS COVERAGE OF HEALTH

At least one-fourth of all articles in daily newspapers are in some way related to health, yet some stories that are considered important by the public health community receive little or no coverage. There is a basic conflict between what gatekeepers judge to be newsworthy and what health specialists believe the public should be told. Basically, the public health community wants positive coverage, it wants its messages used intact, it wants coverage that explains the complexities and uncertainties of science, and it wants illumination of structural-risk factors, rather than a focus on individuals with health problems.

What health communicators often seek to bring to people's attention is healthful behavior and positive role models, which are not particularly newsworthy. Drug abuse coverage is a case illustrating how media and public health priorities seem incompatible. Although journalists have devoted a great deal of time and space to drug problems in recent years, most stories focus on law enforcement and violence, rather than conveying prevention or treatment guidance. Similarly, there is extensive coverage of cancer risks and the dire consequences for patients, but little emphasis on the National Cancer Institute's basic prevention message.

The news media frequently ignore the broad societal issues that are often more significant to public health in favor of more interesting personalized stories about individuals. Wallack (Chapter 2) points out that progress in promoting public health involves social change to correct system failures; however, the media tend to reduce health issues to individual-level concerns and to reinforce existing social and economic arrangements. This emphasis is significant, because the news media play a pivotal role in setting the public agenda and conferring legitimacy on health issues.

In addition to omissions, the news media are criticized for attributing more certainty to new findings than is scientifically justified, for portraying minor advances as major breakthroughs, and for exploiting the emotions of patients and the public.

Nevertheless, public health specialists are increasingly reliant on the news media, due to two key trends in the field. First, as more knowledge is developed about modes of risk reduction, health educators have more messages to convey and more programs to promote. Second, as the healthcare market becomes more highly competitive, institutions need the media to increase their visibility and credibility. According to

Stuyck (Chapter 5), the public health community needs the media more than the media needs the field of public health, producing an imbalanced relationship that may require greater efforts for adaptation on the part of those in public health.

In the past, the public health community has attacked the press on the grounds of its fundamental assumptions and approaches in reporting and editing the news. News professionals regard this stance as unproductive and suggest that health specialists attempt to understand and accept the basic imperative of the decision-making process. They should adapt to the realities of conventional journalistic practice by packaging information in usable form and working cooperatively with media professionals to achieve minor modifications of coverage within the constraints of the current system. In short, the public health community should rethink its approach by taking into account the perspective of the news media gatekeepers who stand between them and the public.

There are a number of journalistic conventions that should be recognized by savvy public health personnel. Meyer (Chapter 3) defines the nature of news and identifies key criteria such as timeliness, geographical proximity, consequences that change or threaten people's lives, human interest, conflict, and unusualness. He also observes that gatekeepers tend to prefer stories that are credible or at least plausible, to fit events and developments into existing constructs, to package information into small and discrete pieces, and to avoid potentially offensive material.

In Chapter 4, Klaidman describes several news logics that apply to health reporting: that there is more coverage of health problems posing a risk to the mass media's core middle-class constituency (which may lead to underemphasis of diseases affecting narrow or powerless segments of the population); that investigative journalism is typically guided by the reporter's strongly held hypothesis (which may lead to rejection of contrary evidence); that new health fads attract the attention of news people; and that economic considerations may undermine coverage (e.g., advertiser influences or large- dollar medical issues).

Some of the limitations inherent in hard-news reporting are less crucial now that print and broadcast media are increasing the level of health service features (e.g., special newspaper health sections, and more frequent inserts in TV news programming). The growing number of science reporters specializing in the health domain has also provided more balance and accuracy. Nevertheless, tensions between health specialists and journalists remain; the conference examined a number of major issues and proposed ideas for improving news coverage of public health.

Media Relations for Health Institutions

Academic institutions traditionally have been wary of the mass media, often devoting resources to publications they can control (such as house organs, magazines, newsletters, and pamphlets), which reach only a limited audience. Increasingly, universities and health centers are recognizing the benefits of public relations to coordinate and shape news media coverage.

These public-relations departments usually focus on soft promotion rather than hard news. In some cases, streams of press releases and engineered media events foster a backlash among journalists, creating rising levels of skepticism. The attempts at institutional control and self-aggrandizement may be undermining the health coverage in the news media. Even the Surgeon General's office is viewed with a skeptical eye; for example, a 1988 report on nutrition was widely regarded as a pseudo-event that was more of an empty public relations effort than an unveiling of new information. The public health community should be cognizant of the news media's wariness about manipulation and cooptation, even for an ostensibly "good" cause such as health education.

On a more technical level, there is a clear need to improve communication skills in institutions, particularly academic medical centers. Public relations specialists must be adept at identifying experts who exhibit media-wise communication abilities and at bringing them together with journalists. Regular contacts between sources and reporters help build a foundation for good health news coverage. For example, an alcohol specialist could meet regularly with a reporter interested in the subject area to talk about a range of new developments and perspectives. This type of interaction not only generates stories directly but provides the reporter with background information to put breaking news into context.

While the increasingly competitive environment faced by public health organizations produces frustration in gaining media access, it may also be fostering greater creativity and cooperation. Institutional competition forces organizations aggressively to pursue new information dissemination techniques, such as video news releases, direct electronic links to newsrooms, and newspaper op-ed pieces. The large number of advocates may help increase overall media coverage of health and highlight specific issues that are the focus of multiple voices. Strains toward greater interinstitutional collaboration may be a beneficial consequence, as organizations jointly develop communication skills training programs, collect audience research information, and implement cooperative campaigns that gain in strength and credibility (e.g., multiorganizational initiatives focusing on the same health problem, or coordination of distinct campaigns targeting the same audience, such as a prevention effort aimed at preventing both drug abuse and early pregnancy among low-income teenagers).

Professional associations and specialized referral services (such as the Science Institute for Public Information) can play an important role in making information more readily available to the news media. Organizations might collaborate in identifying experts and developing background or position papers on particular health issues. One useful service would be computer bulletin boards with telephone numbers of a roster of national or local topical specialists who can be contacted by journalists. Computer networks and bulletin boards are also promising mechanisms for directly accessing facts and commentary on various public health issues.

Health Education Versus Health News

Health promoters and health reporters have conflicting imperatives, seen most clearly in their attitudes toward repetition. Repeated presentation of information is a key to effective health education, but it is the antithesis of news and to a lesser extent soft-feature material. The news media believe that rerunning the same basic themes will produce boredom and lose audiences.

One approach for overcoming this redundancy problem is to treat stories from fresh angles, with health educators seeking to put a new spin on repetitive messages; a variety of news pegs and stimulating perspectives can be used to convey the core educational material. Not only will this increase the likelihood of attracting coverage but it will reawaken audience interest and enhance response to the familiar content. AIDS coverage is an example of effective reporting where hundreds of stories have appeared on different aspects of the problem, with most incorporating the same basic facts about the disease and how it is transmitted.

At a more basic level, health specialists must learn what factors determine the amount of time and space devoted to health topics and what makes a particular story newsworthy to journalists. Greater success can be achieved by providing a human interest slant to stories, creating a visual focus, and personalizing abstract ideas. For example, reporters frame stories around concrete events in the lives of visible individuals, as was the case when Rock Hudson's death dramatically boosted AIDS coverage. However, news is a perishable commodity, and a disparate series of events and developments is required to keep the fundamental story alive; in the case of AIDS, the Hudson news was followed by storylines about infected school children and then the spread among heterosexuals.

Those in the health field should also recognize the important differences in the interests and capabilities of various media, such as national versus local outlets and TV versus radio versus newspapers versus magazines. Depending on the channel and the audience it reaches, health educators must adjust by emphasizing different topics, angles, levels of complexity, degrees of brevity, and styles of information presentation.

Specialists in the public health field can facilitate educational treatment of complex material by providing clearcut, black-and-white guidance information to reporters. This requires more aggressive efforts at reaching consensus within the field in identifying magnitude of risks and formulating recommended guidelines. For example, after considerable controversy and compromise by experts, the National Institutes of Health established 200 as the cutoff point for a "safe" cholesterol level, so this simple figure could readily be disseminated to the public.

On the other hand, controversy among scientists or health care providers does serve the function of generating news and keeping a health issue high on the agenda. The news value of conflict is served by differences in opinion and contradictory evidence, as has happened in debates over the dimensions and treatments for diseases such as AIDS.

The standard public relations practice of establishing working relationships with gatekeepers can also provide the groundwork for gaining improved coverage of public health issues. Getting editors and reporters interested in an issue or problem may pay dividends in the long run, especially if they decide to champion a particular cause. While cultivation of personal contacts helps achieve this end, health promoters might also seek to motivate journalists with more pragmatic professional inducements, such as awards or commendation letters to individuals and media organizations for excellence in covering certain subjects. An awards program is most likely to be successful if sponsored by highly credible institutions, associations, or societies, rather than by special-interest groups that might be perceived as manipulative in recognizing favored journalists.

Media advocacy is an innovative approach for aggressively promoting health causes, particularly public policy reforms. Advocates seek to generate news coverage that will serve to reframe public debate on societal issues. In Chapter 11, Wallack describes emerging news advocacy techniques that have proven effective in advancing nonprofit causes, and he urges application to the public health field. A key method is "creative epidemiology," in which factual data about prevalence of health problems is packaged in an interesting and meaningful manner. The method of "issue framing" focuses attention on problematic industry practices in order to shift blame away from the individual and to delegitimatize corporations that make unhealthy products.

Media advocacy practitioners employ a variety of publicity techniques for attracting media attention, such as conducting novel and provocative research studies, generating controversy, and staging unconventional pseudoevents. For example, when an adolescent pregnancy prevention PSA was rejected as offensive by the TV networks, the sponsoring organization held a press conference to treat this rejection as a news event; this drew greater attention to the content of the message, and the PSA was carried as a news item on evening newscasts.

Clearly, there is a need for health educators to learn more about dealing with the news media. Media awareness courses in public health schools would help promote understanding and sensitivity and build better skills. Short training courses for people working in government, medical and scientific organizations would also be helpful. Stuyck (Chapter 5) presents a set of recommendations for improved communication practices by health educators, based on a survey of experienced news gatekeepers. The media advocacy principles presented by Wallack in Chapter 11 are pertinent to the public health community; health policy professionals might be trained in these advocacy techniques and supplied with materials for local adaptation, perhaps from a national resource center.

There is also room for improvement on the part of the news media. For working journalists, periodic seminars on public health subjects is a promising approach. For better training of prospective writers on health issues, both journalism schools and public health schools can develop special courses and fellowships that promote responsible and effective science writing. In particular, news professionals need to gain a broader and deeper understanding of health in order to put stories into their proper context. Journalists should learn to discriminate between pure and applied scientists as sources, because of the differing levels of practical and policy-relevant information each type is willing or able to provide. Reporters should be trained to present health information clearly, not simplistically; the audience can comprehend complex topics that are carefully explained. Another priority is the education of editors; their lack of appreciation for the public's interest in health matters is a significant obstacle to expanding coverage.

A final barrier to be surmounted is the ignorance and apathy of the general public. A long-term effort is needed to raise people's knowledge and understanding of health-related issues, problems, and solutions, beginning in the schools. This will create more demand for higher quality news media coverage and facilitate learning from the content that is provided. In the meantime, both news personnel and public health specialists need to focus more clearly on producing coverage of newsworthy aspects of specific health topics about which the public is currently uninformed or misinformed. Based on surveys of the general population and priority target groups, key gaps in knowledge should be identified and addressed in publicity efforts.

HEALTH-RELATED ENTERTAINMENT PORTRAYALS

Television is our society's primary storyteller and most important agent of informal socialization. Television's health-related themes are presented daily to an overwhelming majority of the population; entertainment viewing totals three hours per day, with children and the elderly watching the most programming. Both positive and negative health images and information are prominently and repeatedly woven into the plotlines of popular programs. Systematic content analyses have delineated the following array of portrayals that are intentionally or unintentionally featured in soap operas, sitcoms, prime-time dramas, and other types of programming:

Physical illness is a central event in many television stories; the ill person has an aura of goodness and typically gets better. There is almost no mention of costs, insurance, or the health care system as a whole. Physicians are very powerful and competent authority figures, surrounded by deferential nurses and paramedics; other health professionals are absent. Mental illness is a sinister and frightening phenomenon, often involving aggression and failure. Violence is far more common than in the real world, but pain, suffering, and medical help rarely follow. Sex is increasingly pervasive and titillating, but prevention of pregnancy or disease is seldom incorporated into the plot. AIDS is a scientific mystery, a gay issue, and a political story. Alcohol use is widespread, especially during personal crisis. Smoking is rare, but so is quitting smoking; currently TV seems to ignore the issue completely, allowing smokers to escape from reality. Illegal drug use is also infrequent, but it carries negative consequences and is usually depicted in the context of law enforcement.

Barriers to Improving Health Portrayals

Health educators would like to see the entertainment media deal with health subject-matter more frequently and more realistically, but two basic obstacles are evident. First, television's priority for attracting and satisfying large audiences is not compatible with educational objectives. In dealing with health portrayals, program creators can make only minor adaptations (e.g., occasionally modifying an unhealthy depiction or inserting a prohealth comment) without sacrificing the enjoyment value of their offerings. Montgomery (Chapter 9) describes how advocacy groups have successfully influenced entertainment gatekeepers by confining suggestions to a narrow range of easily accommodated adjustments. TV executives resist requests for extensive changes that might undermine audience share and thus lose commercial support.

A second barrier involves the networks' policies of self-censorship in "editorializing" on controversial or taboo subjects, such as abortion, birth control, smoke-free environments, or health care reforms. Even when it comes to less controversial issues, there is a tendency to be very cautious in treating aspects that are considered sensitive to certain segments of viewers. One central concern is offending commercial sponsors with direct interests in the health domain, particularly alcohol companies and food/tobacco conglomerates. Pressure is also brought to bear by special-interest groups, such as medical associations that seek to control the content of physician/hospital dramas, and organizations crusading to eliminate sexual, violent, or immoral content.

Opportunities

Over the years, there have been certain TV programs that dealt with significant social issues, usually as a result of a key gatekeeper's championship. The champion can be a producer, executive, writer, or performer who feels a strong commitment to the issue. In the deregulatory climate, there is more freedom for these individuals to promote a favorite cause.

Networking and personal contacts are important in getting more and better health messages into entertainment programming. For example, a model public relations effort is the Harvard School of Public Health's collaboration with Hollywood producers to incorporate the "designated driver" concept into scripts. This followed the pioneering initiative of Breed and De Foe (1982) to employ "cooperative consultation" techniques in working with writers to improve the portrayal of proper drinking practices. This topic is explored more fully in the chapter by Montgomery.

Certain industry-based organizations have endeavored to promote socially responsible programming. The Entertainment Industries Council has successfully advocated changes in the depiction of alcohol and drug use and safe driving, and the Television Academy of Arts and Sciences Outreach Program has asked producers to place more emphasis on showing the consequences of risky behavior. An important philosophical issue concerns the appropriateness of the entertainment industry's "social engineering" of selected health and safety practices, such as the designated driver, protected sex, safety belt buckling, nonsmoking, and nutritional habits.

It should be noted that in other countries, entire TV series have been created to convey prosocial and health content. One recent example was the popular Indian soap opera *Hum Log*, which integrated development-related themes such as family planning and equal status for women into entertaining plots that attracted broad audiences (Singhal & Rogers, 1989). The practice of blending entertainment and education is also exemplified by the use of rock music as a vehicle for promoting teenage sexual abstinence via recordings and music videos. Entertainment-education campaigns must be careful not to make the educational message too blatant or hard sell, or they will not attract a sufficient number of viewers and listeners.

In order to enhance the treatment of health under the current constraints of the U.S. system, a first important step is to make entertainment gatekeepers more aware of health issues and public health professionals more aware of media needs. Before effectively educating the public, individuals working in both fields must themselves become better educated about the processes and priorities of the other field. The public health community ought to be more sensitive to the realities of the media; mass communicators should be more aware of the public's fascination with health and more cognizant of the influence they have on the audience and the value of presenting appropriate health behaviors and consequences. This can be facilitated by high-level networking between leading figures from both camps and greater interaction among public health and entertainment media organizations. In addition to the major broadcast networks, efforts should focus on independent production companies, cable networks, and movie studios.

In implementing efforts to alter the portrayal of health in the entertainment media, decisionmakers must give prime consideration to determining which types of content are most problematic and which portrayals should be emphasized. An illustration of this strategic issue can be raised in the case of alcohol and drunk driving. Although alcohol is widely consumed by TV characters, the sheer pervasiveness of drinking is probably less critical than the mixture of motivations and consequences. Whether viewers see 100 or 200 drinking acts per week may not make much of a difference, but the ratio of positive versus negative depictions can significantly determine attitudinal and behavioral outcomes (e.g., downplaying deficit motives for drinking and more realistically representing the harmful consequences involving drinking and/or driving). Increased modeling of certain responsible behaviors would also be beneficial (e.g., declining drinks, choosing nonalcoholic beverages, discontinuing before intoxication, and intervening to prevent drunkenness or drunk driving).

In addition to content changes, efforts are needed to teach the public to be more discriminating consumers of entertainment portrayals. This should involve both sensitization to the positive health messages available in the media and inoculation against dysfunctional influences.

EFFECTIVE INFORMATION CAMPAIGN STRATEGIES

In recent years, health topics such as drug abuse, drunk driving, smoking, and AIDS have dominated the public service time and space made available by the mass media. Indeed, President George Bush asked that the media disseminate $1 million worth of antidrug messages per day in 1990. Some state government agencies and private associations have begun to purchase time and space for their health messages.

Most of these education and persuasion efforts sponsored by health organizations and private-public partnerships are designed as systematic *campaigns*, defined by Flay and Burton (Chapter 10) as "an integrated series of communication activities, using multiple operations and channels, aimed at populations or target audiences, usually of long duration, with a clear purpose." Campaign design must be based on a fundamental understanding of how the media operate, how messages can influence the audience, and how these campaigns fit within the commercial mass media environment.

According to the exploration of theory and practice in the chapter by Flay and Burton, there are seven necessary conditions for campaign effectiveness: (1) developing high-quality messages, sources, and channels through needs assessment, application of theory, and formative research; (2) disseminating the stimuli to target audiences frequently and consistently for a sustained period; (3) attracting the attention of the potential receivers; (4) encouraging favorable interpersonal communication about the issue; (5) changing the awareness, knowledge, opinions, attitudes, feelings, normative beliefs, intentions, skills, and/or behaviors of individuals; (6) causing societal change with supplemental community and government changes; and (7) accumulating systematic knowledge about the conditions of maximum impact through summative evaluation.

Campaign strategies can be improved in a number of ways. Concepts and principles from the fields of mass communication and social marketing should be refined and implemented by health campaign designers. Innovative stylistic approaches should be employed in packaging campaign information in a more attractive, relevant, and understandable manner. Special attention must be devoted to developing more effective persuasive appeals that will convince target audiences to change health-related attitudes and behaviors. Modes beyond the standard TV PSA should be utilized more extensively, including approaches that rely on the other three types of media content that have already been described: arranging for pro-health advertisements (e.g., cooperative partnerships with private corporations), generating news coverage and feature stories (e.g., public relations and media advocacy, especially via creatively staged pseudoevents that promote campaign themes), and incorporating campaign material in entertainment programming. In addition, a portion of campaign materials ought to be allocated to countermessages that inoculate young people against undue influence from problematic themes and depictions in ads and entertainment programming.

The creation of an applied handbook for campaign design would make a major contribution. This document could incorporate social marketing principles, persuasive strategy guidelines, and evaluation research techniques in a practical package that could be utilized at national, state, and local levels to improve the effectiveness of public-service information campaigns. Another valuable resource would be a standardized health message testing service, where rough or finished PSAs and print messages could be evaluated to determine effectiveness before mass dissemination. In addition, a national resource center could be created as a repository for health messages, providing a source of ideas for new materials or local adaptations.

A final issue concerns the funding for information campaign messages and services. Given the declining availability of free placement, there is a need to develop financial resources that would enable production of the highest quality public-service spots for the scarce slots still available, and would permit purchase of desirable time and space for health messages that do not receive donated placement in the media. Suggestions include an excise tax on unhealthful products to support health promotion, federal financing of paid messages, governmentally mandated placement of countermessages (particularly in the case of drinking and smoking), and more reliance on state government initiatives.

MEDIA AND HEALTH: RESEARCH PRIORITIES

In the past decade, there has been a rapid expansion of academic research examining mass communication and public health. This has reflected the growth of scholarly interest in the broader field of health communication, which led to the inauguration of the new journal *Health Communication* in 1989. While much has been learned, there remains a rich and diverse array of phenomena to be studied in the 1990s. This closing section will sketch an agenda for researchers interested in investigating the role of the mass media in the public health domain.

Before outlining research topics, it is important to emphasize the subject of research utilization. Because health communication data have significant practical implications, investigators must consider modes of dissemination beyond the preparation of standard academic papers and publications. There are a number of "target audiences" besides fellow scholars: health professionals (especially individuals who deal with the news media or those who design communication campaign strategies), government personnel (including health agency staffers who plan communication programs, officials at regulatory agencies responsible for media and advertising policies, and legislative decisionmakers who enact regulations and fund programs), leaders of media industry and trade associations (such as broadcast/cable companies, news organizations, advertising associations, entertainment councils, and associations of corporations marketing health-related products and services, each of whom may develop codes or self-regulatory guidelines and implement pertinent public service projects).

In order effectively to reach these professional audiences, research information must be repackaged in a usable form; in addition to making the findings readily understandable, researchers may want to draw strategic implications and perhaps undertake advocacy efforts. Indeed, an important research priority is to study the health research dissemination process, focusing on the most effective approaches for translating empirical data and theoretical ideas into practical inputs for those on the front lines.

Related to this point, there is a need for investigations of health media gatekeepers. Relatively little is known about the creative and decision-making practices of journalists who report and edit health news, magazine writers who prepare feature stories, TV doctors who present health advice, entertainment media personnel who write and produce fictional scripts involving health-related storylines and portrayals, broadcast public service directors who select PSAs for airplay, and public relations practitioners who develop publicity releases or devise pseudoevents in the public health arena.

For example, several specific research questions about the news gatekeeping process are worth pursuing: To what extent are decisions about news influenced by editors' perceptions of audience interest in health matters? How does the journalists' level of understanding of health shape their decisionmaking? What factors play a role in keeping a health story "alive" over time?

Finally, it would be valuable to conduct critical studies examining media economy and the interrelationships among government regulators, advertisers and producers, and the mass media industry as applied to health issues.

Content Analysis Research

One of the most popular types of mass communication research is content analysis, which systematically measures the quantity and nature of mediated messages. Health-related content in conventional media channels appears in news stories, advertisements, entertainment portrayals, and public service messages. Signorielli (Chapter 8) describes the substantial content analytic literature that focuses on television entertainment programming. This focus should be broadened to measure what is being presented beyond the confines of network TV series. There is a need to chart the dimensions of these relatively neglected types of content: hard news in TV newscasts and newspapers (a substantial portion of all news items relate to public health, with prominent coverage of topics such as AIDS, drug abuse, drunk driving, environmental hazards, and violent crime), the informational features in the print and broadcast media (e.g., newspaper advice and other syndicated columns, magazine articles, television doctor segments, and radio talk show interviews), advertising for a broad array of commercial products and services that affect health (e.g., alcoholic beverages, cigarettes, foods, proprietary medicines, fitness centers, diet programs, and medical care facilities), and the traditional public information and education campaigns (e.g., broadcast PSAs and print public service ads).

In analyzing media health content, several different purposes and methodological approaches are relevant. The most primitive technique involves *simple counts*, measuring various message dimensions for a specified content domain (e.g., number of alcoholic drinks per hour on prime-time dramas in a given TV season, or quantity of front page stories about various facets of the AIDS problem in selected prestige newspapers). When collected over time, these data can form the basis for the tracking of trends (e.g., increasing or decreasing number of anti-drug PSAs across a five-year period). These quantitative assessments serve an important monitoring function, providing precise descriptive information for policymakers and advocates who are interested in the changing nature of media depictions of public health.

Content analysis findings can also be used to draw inferences about *performance of sources* (e.g., determining whether cigarette advertisers are complying with self-regulatory code provisions, identifying which types of quotes or "sound bites" are favored by journalists covering the health beat, assessing the accuracy of health content, and examining whether fictional portrayals created by entertainment producers reflect the current shape of public opinion and changing prevalence rates of health problems in society).

Entertainment content analysts should augment traditional character/ act description by examining how the fictional stories are structured. It would be valuable to know how health issues are woven into plots and what function they serve. These *structural and contextual* aspects of televised presentations can provide useful qualitative information for interpreting the simple count data.

While these types of content information are valuable, the highest priority should be given to analyses of message attributes that are sensitive to potential *audience effects*. In developing measures, researchers should take into account key theoretical mechanisms that determine the direction and degree of impact on viewers, listeners, and readers. For example, *social learning* theory directs attention to the characteristics of mediated role models and the depiction of reinforcements for certain behavior patterns (thus, the number of drinks per hour may be less significant than the attractiveness of drinkers and the positive or negative consequences portrayed); the *cognitive response* model suggests that the potential for audience counterarguing should be considered in measuring health claims in persuasive messages; and the *agenda-setting* perspective broadens the measurement focus to take into account the prominence of news item positioning as well as total quantity.

Audience Effects

With few exceptions, very little research has been conducted to assess the impact of health-related content on the public. Thus, the field is wide open for researchers who want to investigate the broad range of audience responses to various types of messages.

Before discussing the effects on those exposed to health messages, it is important first to consider the factors that determine exposure. Although there is a great deal of media content conveying health information and persuasion, it is apparent that people pay attention to a relatively small proportion of available material. This exposure barrier is especially a problem for news and public service messages, which are largely ignored or avoided by many segments of the population. Researchers should explore the range of needs, interests, and tastes that motivate individuals to select health messages encountered in the media, and identify the reasons for nonexposure or inattentiveness. A better understanding of the determinants of exposure would be extremely valuable for advising message producers on how to improve the substantive and stylistic message qualities in order to attract larger audiences.

In assessing the actual impact, there is a diverse array of outcome variables that can be measured beyond the standard criteria of awareness and attitude change. At the cognitive level, researchers should examine the acquisition of *applied knowledge* that is relevant to the individual's personal health situation (e.g., learning useful information to cope with a problem), the formation of mental *images* of health-related concepts, objects, and roles (e.g., products, life-styles, victims, or care providers), the development of *perceptions* about real-world phenomena (e.g., perceived prevalence of certain practices or diseases, or conceptions about the social and economic origins of public health problems), the creation of personal *beliefs* about the consequences of health-related behaviors (e.g., risk probabilities), and alterations in agenda *salience* levels (e.g., relative significance of various public health problems facing society, or importance of certain consequences of behaviors).

At the affective level, researchers can measure *interest* in health subjects, *preferences* among health-related products, and critical *evaluation* skills for processing health claims and portrayals. Besides attitudinal conversion, investigations can also examine the creation, reinforcement, and maintenance of *attitudes, opinions, and values* (e.g., forming an opinion on a new health issue, strengthening an existing attitude, or preserving a healthy value in the face of social pressures).

Since the ultimate outcomes occur at the behavioral level, researchers must assess these overt variables even though the degree of impact may be less pronounced than for cognitive and affective orientations. For fundamental health *practices* that are unlikely to change dramatically in response to a single media stimulus, there is a need for measurement that utilizes highly sensitive scaling or that assesses cumulative impact over a long period of exposure to multiple messages. Behaviors other than personal practices can also be examined, such as interpersonal *discussion* of health topics and social *interventions* to influence the actions of other people.

In addition to research focusing on individual effects, investigators should broaden the scope of analysis to include higher-order aggregations (e.g., impact on couples, families, groups, organizations, and communities) and differential responses across segments of the population (e.g., social categories based on age, gender, race, social class, and health status). This sociologically oriented type of research provides ecologically valid assessment of media influence and permits specification of the unequal distribution of effects among subgroups (e.g., knowledge gaps due to differences in health message access, exposure, processing, or learning).

In selecting research topics, many academic researchers will be attracted to theoretically interesting phenomena based on personal preferences. For those who want to conduct applied studies, there are several domains of health-related content where effects research is particularly needed to guide policymakers and message designers. Suggested examples will be offered in the areas of advertising, news, entertainment, and public service campaigns.

The priority issues in advertising involve the impact of TV commercials and print ads for problematic products such as alcohol, tobacco, over-the-counter and prescription drugs, and food products. Research is needed to determine the degree of advertising influence on consumption of these substances among vulnerable segments of the population. Investigators should also seek to isolate the specific types of appeals that may contribute to unhealthy consumption patterns or other deleterious effects (e.g., women's liberation imagery in cigarette ads, or nutrition claims in food ads). On the other hand, studies can examine whether certain types of advertising practices produce positive effects (e.g., private-public cooperative ads, or ads containing warning labels). More generally, little is known about how the consumer processes information from advertising relative to other information sources (e.g., weight given to commercial claims versus news items or public service messages).

The topic that has generated the greatest current controversy is the impact of alcohol advertising on drunk driving, where additional research could help provide answers to the following questions: Is there a clear connection between alcohol advertising and drunk driving behavior, particularly among youthful drivers? If so, what changes in the nature of advertising practices would reduce drinking by drivers (or driving by drinkers)? Would a ban on broadcast advertising lead to less drinking (and thus reduce the incidence of drunk driving)? Would the elimination of vehicle portrayals in ads help minimize problematic effects? Should advertisers disclose safety risks involved in consuming their products in a driving context? Would it be beneficial if ads depicted positive role modeling, such as drivers refusing drinks or companions intervening to discourage excessive drinking or prevent drunk driving?

In the news domain, applied research would be helpful in determining how different forms of packaging information facilitate audience response: Should there be more simplified treatment or greater detail? How much redundancy in presenting basic ideas is optimum? Are colorful bites informative or just interesting? Does the emphasis on dire risks motivate people to change their behavior or does it produce denial? Should stories stress statistics or personalized cases to get the point across? What is the impact of sensationalized treatment of health news? What types of coverage generated by media advocacy practitioners are influential? How important is the source of the news story?

As indicated by Signorielli (Chapter 8), there is a dearth of research on almost all types of entertainment media effects. In addition to delineating the influence of the standard portrayals of doctors, diseases, and healthy/unhealthy role models, applied research would be useful in exploring the impact of innovative programming such as designated driver inserts, episodes dedicated to a prohealth theme, and real-life medical reenactment series.

Some of the entertainment effects research should be qualitative, with exploratory studies examining the process of engagement in fictional stories and the way viewers understand and interpret the stream of images that they view.

For information campaigns, much remains to be learned about the relative effectiveness of various sources, channels, and message styles, formats and appeals (especially fear appeals). The most useful avenue for improving effectiveness of campaign messages is formative evaluation research (Atkin & Freimuth, 1989). Preproduction research and message pretesting provide campaign strategists and message producers with valuable information for decisions along each step of the design process from identifying target audiences to refining rough executions. Formative research has played an instrumental role in the success of a number of recent health campaigns, such as the programs described by Flay and Burton (Chapter 10) and the federal *Be Smart, Don't Start* campaign aimed at pre-drinkers.

However, this type of research is used almost exclusively for imme-diate decision making in a narrow campaign context. There have been few attempts to review more broadly what generalizations are emerging from multiple investigations of particular populations (e.g., preadoles-cents, low-income minorities) by various campaign sponsors, or what are the "lessons learned" about particular strategy variables (e.g., mes-sage styles, or source characteristics) across many years of message pretesting research.

CONCLUSION

A major goal of the agencies sponsoring the media and health conference is the creation of a shared agenda for cooperation between mass media and public health professionals in addressing the issues and challenges of communicating health information to the public. There are a number of complexities and conflicts involved in this process, due to differences in objectives, philosophies, conventions, and capabilities between the two fields; there are also remarkable diversity and compe-tition within the public health community, and the "mass media" are far from monolithic, with a wide variety of channels, outlets, and formats.

Further, there is a diverse array of health topics of compelling interest and public need. Health messages are generally complicated, and the media most frequently offer too limited time or space to cover the subjects adequately. The health community has traditionally relied on free public service campaigns to reach the population, but the amount of time and space for nondrug messages is dwindling. Public health organizations are experimenting with paid advertising, more sophisticated public relations and media advocacy practices, and coop-erative efforts with private companies and entertainment producers to disseminate their messages. At the same time, commercial advertis-ers are aggressively promoting health-related products through the media, and they are increasingly relying on health claims to persuade consumers.

In this complex and dynamic context, there is a variety of approaches that can be pursued to more effectively educate the public about health. A report summarizing the discussions at the conference (*Mass Media and Health: Opportunities for Improving the Nation's Health*, 1990) proposes the following recommendations for the public health community:

(1) Educate public health specialists regarding the opportunities and the restrictions in using the media to communicate health messages to the public, including the multiple facets (e.g., public service and paid advertising, news, public affairs, and entertainment) and differences between channels (e.g., TV, radio, newspapers, magazines).

(2) Identify common interests among health organizations (such as a specific health issue or target audience) and form informal coalitions to increase "clout" with the media.

(3) Seek media cooperation at all levels, from corporate leadership to individual reporters, through personal contacts; establish and nurture contacts over time, not just in regard to a specific health need; and seek their involvement in program planning stages to interest them in the cause or problem, not just the message.

(4) Increase outreach efforts to the minority media to convince them of the compelling needs of their audience for health information, and the interest of their audiences in health.

(5) Work with schools of journalism and professional associations to provide science and health training to journalists, and to develop guidelines for reporting health and science issues, thus increasing the depth of understanding, raising the level of skepticism, and refining the judgment with which journalists prepare stories about these complex issues.

(6) Establish mechanisms such as a computer bulletin board to provide journalists with quick access to health spokespersons, background information, and the positions of pertinent health agencies on specific issues.

(7) Recognize the conflicts as well as the convergences in interests between public health and the mass media; set clear, realistic expectations for health programs involving the media, and solicit broad participation by the media and support from corporations that advertise through the media.

(8) Develop guidelines for collaboration between industry and the health community to direct and safeguard cooperative advertising and other media ventures, and develop guidelines for promoting product health claims.

(9) Plan data collection and program tracking for all media efforts, to increase what is known about the effects of communicating about health through the media.

(10) Support the establishment of media resource centers to share effective media materials, including PSAs; to maintain contacts with journalists; and to share advice and case studies illustrating effective media strategies.

(11) Educate the public (especially children) to be informed consumers of health information in the mass media, including product health claims, conflicting news reports, and the complexities of fast-breaking scientific findings.

A recurring theme expressed by media representatives at the conference is the need to recognize that the mass media are not obligated to educate the consumer about health. It is incumbent on the public health community, as one of many interests groups seeking cooperation of the media, to understand the motivations of media gatekeepers, to convince them of the importance of covering health issues, and to initiate collaborative ventures. The remaining chapters of this book will elaborate the conflicts and complexities and explore possible avenues of cooperation in advancing the health communication agenda.

2

Mass Media and Health Promotion:
Promise, Problem, and Challenge

LAWRENCE WALLACK

What is the role of the mass media in promoting the health of the public? There are greatly divergent viewpoints on this issue. On one end there are those who believe that if only we could get the right message to the right people in the right way at the right time, then even the most intractable public health problem would yield. The golden bullet of this approach is the catchy slogan (e.g., Just say no!), and the applicator is not a hypodermic needle but a television set.

On the other end are those who believe the mass media to be a malevolent force that is actually a barrier to health education. Media institutions are presumed to be driven by profit and the need to round up the greatest number of consumers to sell to advertisers. Consumption is viewed as the germ that undermines the health of the public, and the business of television is the vector through which it is transmitted. This perspective argues that media outlets exist primarily to meet the needs of the advertisers by stimulating higher levels of consumption. Public service is a very low priority.

A third argument is that mass media have no effect on individual behavior. This "null effects" hypothesis suggests that the media strictly reinforce rather than shape public opinion and individual behavior. The

AUTHOR'S NOTE: I would like to thank Linda Nettekoven, Meredith Minkler, and Robert Denniston for their helpful comments on this chapter.

mass media are viewed as part of the general environment but not as change agents or targets of change.

Each of these perspectives has serious drawbacks. The first is based on questionable assumptions that lead to interventions with little value, the second leads to an unproductive nihilism, while the third perspective has little credibility and is clearly contradicted by recent mass communication research.

The appropriate role of the mass media in addressing public health issues must be found in a broadly manufactured middle ground. There is no denying that the mass media have moments of brilliance. *Hill Street Blues* and *Cagney and Lacey* on alcoholism, *St. Elsewhere*, *Designing Women* and *LA Law* on AIDS, *Valerie* on birth control, and *Family Ties* on a number of relevant issues are but a few examples. Well-designed and -implemented media campaigns have been shown to be useful for recruiting people into community health programs (Levenkron & Farquhar, 1982), stimulate use of a cancer hot- line number, increase purchase of high-fiber cereals (Levy & Stokes, 1987) and, in some cases, reduce smoking (Flay, 1987b). It is now reasonable to anticipate at least limited effects from carefully designed comprehensive public communication campaigns. However, the scarcity of successful campaigns and the infrequency of serious treatment of public health issues on television serve as reminders of the drabness and limitations of the vast television landscape from a health perspective.

While there is excitement in the unrealized potential of the mass media, there is sufficient basis for very serious concern regarding the possibly counterproductive effects on public health. The mass media may not tell people what to think, but they clearly do tell people what to think about. The media help set the discussion agenda for society and create the boundaries within which debate takes place. The media tend to reinforce conventional definitions of health problems and hence determine, to a large extent, the legitimacy of various solutions. Conventional definitions that have led to unsuccessful approaches are tried repeatedly with little success. While public health problems are, to a large extent, socially generated, the mass media reinforce individual-level explanations. This focus deflects attention away from causes and social conditions, highlighting instead symptoms and personal failures.

The mass media, in a sense, provide society with a menu from which strategies for health promotion are selected. Part of developing realistic expectations about the role of mass media in health promotion is better to understand how presentation of issues by the mass media can act as both a barrier and a facilitator. In this way perhaps we can make better use of the invaluable resource that the mass media represent.

THE PROMISE

The promise of mass media is to facilitate the goals of a democratic society by providing a forum for a diversity of opinion and information. Viewed idealistically, the objective is to empower citizens better to make decisions about how to contribute to community life as well as their own individual well-being. The mass media approach this promise through news and public service messages and also, in many ways, through entertainment programming (e.g., provision of positive role models).

Americans read, watch, and listen to a broad range of mass media. Yet for all the newspapers, magazines, and radio stations, television is America's primary medium. On any given evening, between 91.7 million and 103.8 million people are watching their televisions (Nielsen Media Research, 1987).

From early childhood through high school, television viewing consumes more time that any other single activity except sleeping. For adults, only hours spent working and sleeping exceed television viewing. Television is generally seen as the most credible media source. It has become America's primary source of news. When asked which medium they would believe if conflicting or different stories were being reported, half of the public reports they would believe the television version, compared to one-fourth who would believe the newspaper (TIO/Roper, 1989). In a study conducted for General Mills, Yankelovich, Skelly, and White, Inc. (1979) found that after "doctors and dentists," television programs were listed as the main source of health information. Those more poorly informed about health issues were more likely to rely on television as a main source of health information.

Research on public communication campaigns has produced findings emphasizing the potential of this approach for improving the health of the public. For example, Flay (1987b) argues that mass-mediated smoking cessation programs, even if only producing success rates of a few percent, can result in thousands of new nonsmokers at a relatively low cost. Others (e.g., Solomon, 1982; Mendelsohn, 1973) suggest that the mass media approach is fundamentally sound but the application is faulty. In other words, if used at a level consistent with our knowledge about what works, public communication campaigns can have a beneficial effect on health status.

In general, many researchers agree that public communication campaigns can play an important role in communicating information to the public, placing health on the public's agenda, and contributing to changing lifestyle behaviors (e.g., O'Keefe & Reid-Nash, 1986; Flay, 1987a; Atkin, 1981; Maccoby & Alexander, 1980; Solomon, 1982; McGuire, 1984). The potential for positive effects appears to be enhanced through better application of formative research, more attention to problem definition, more detailed audience analysis, realistic goal setting, supplementation with local-level activity, and better use of theory and previous research. In sum, one communication scholar argues that the contemporary public communication campaign is more effective than those of earlier decades because of increased comprehensiveness, overall better planning, and the fall from vogue of engineering and regulatory strategies (Paisley, 1981).

THE PROBLEM

The primary problem that the public health advocate faces when trying to use the mass media to promote health is the fundamental link between the public's health and the social structure. The pursuit of public health goals often involves social change; the public health perspective primarily emphasizes system failures to explain poor health. The mass media, for the most part, reinforce existing arrangements and primarily emphasize failures of individuals to behave appropriately as an explanation of poor health.

Orwell's *1984* predicted a world of complete and clear control. The powerful images of *1984* have become a part of our cultural understanding, a reference point shared by many. But Neil Postman (1985) argues that this fixation on Orwell neglects the dangers presented in Huxley's *Brave New World*:

> What Orwell feared were those who would ban books. What Huxley feared was that there would be no reason to ban a book, for there would be no one who wanted to read one. Orwell feared those who would deprive us of information. Huxley feared those who would give us so much that we would be reduced to passivity and egoism. Orwell feared the truth would be concealed from us. Huxley feared the truth would be drowned in a sea of irrelevance. (Postman, 1985, p. vi)

Postman's analysis has serious implications for health promotion efforts. The abundance and sometimes poor quality of health information in our environment potentially trivializes health issues by focusing on personal habits and the sole responsibility of the individual. Whether the information is generated by news, regular programming, or health education campaigns, attention is usually deflected away from social and political factors. The need for a quick fix, for simple cause-and-effect explanations, and for clear assignment of responsibility tend to promote clarity and conciseness of the message but does little to enhance understanding or uncover the true nature of public health problems. Trivialization involves three systematic processes: reduction of health issues to individual-level concerns; promotion of consumer products without attention to public health concerns; and, reinforcement of existing social and economic arrangements.

Reduction of Health Issues to Individual-Level Concerns

Mass media are well suited to messages that flow from a life-style theory of health promotion. Just as life-style theory tends to reduce complex health issues to individual behaviors, television takes social and health issues and reduces them to personal emotional dramas. Problems are ultimately defined as a lack of information or as people with the right information making the wrong decisions. The individual drinks too much, takes drugs, or fails to eat the right foods simply because he or she does not know better. The logic of the remedy suggests that if we could just get the right information to the right people, each one of them would change and eventually the larger social problem would be diminished. Reason would win out! For a select part of the population this logic may well apply. Yet, for the vast majority, this is an inadequate and partial strategy.

Public health problems are linked to social conditions and have strong economic and political components. One of the most consistent research findings in public health is the strong relationship between social class and disease. Social class, not individual behavior or medical care, is the best predictor of illness. For example, one of the most powerful predictors of morbidity and mortality experience is income—persons in lower social-economic classes have higher rates of virtually every disease (e.g., Marmot, Kogevinas, & Elston, 1987; Syme & Berkman, 1981). This kind of information has serious practical and political implications, yet popular media seldom present such issues.

People who watch more television are more likely to have a generally conservative view of health and medicine. For example, heavy viewers are more likely to be complacent about eating, drinking, and exercise, to have high confidence in physicians, and to be uninterested in prevention. This antiprevention bias is not surprising. When treatment modalities are shown, they tend to be drugs or machines and have a heavy biomedical emphasis (Turow & Coe, 1985). The quick fix in programming seems consistent with the quick fix themes of television commercials and the all too frequent heroic surgery or "miracle drug" news reporting.

Overall, television programming tends to present us with a picture of disease as an individual issue that is located at the family level and dealt with either in a mechanical way or as an informational problem. As a network executive quoted by Gitlin (1983, p. 179) noted, "The networks are always mistaking real social issues for little human condition stories." Gerbner, Morgan, and Signorielli (1982, p. 305) sum up television portrayals of health, "The cultivation of ignorance and neglect, especially among the otherwise relatively enlightened viewers, coupled with an unrealistic belief in the magic of medicine, is likely to perpetuate unhealthy life-styles. . . . and frustrate efforts at health education."

In sum, television in general reduces social and health issues to individual level problems (see also Montgomery, Chapter 9). The social roots of health problems are usually trivialized or ignored. There is a failure to question the social arrangements that contribute to the problem, ignoring such crucial facts as the relationship between poverty and disease. While public discussion about the problem may be stimulated, television's limited treatment of the problem insures that basic understanding about causes and solutions is not enhanced.

Promotion of Products Without Concern for Public Health

Advertising, as a primary instrument of promotion, has profound effects on our society. It is the economic basis for the operation of the mass media. As such, advertising is an invisible hand that gently influences a wide range of editorial decisions regarding how health-related issues are covered. Also, advertising provides a barrage of information, often with health implications, that frequently runs counter to public health goals.

Health education campaigns generally provide a message of thought-fulness, moderation, and restraint in life-style. Advertising, on the other hand, is the drum major of consumption, promoting higher levels of consumption of potentially health-compromising products through life-style appeals. Campaigns urging people to "Just say no!" to drugs, sex, alcohol, or another helping of dessert are surrounded by attractive role models extolling the virtues of no restraint. Even a brief review of print and electronic media would lead one to think that the national slogan is "Go for it!"

The general life-style and values that advertising promotes are infinitely more important than the marketing of any specific product. When advertising is a life-style promoter, and when that life-style is linked to a number of acute and chronic health problems, it is of utmost concern to the health professional.

Many media critics have pointed out that advertising cannot be separated from the entertainment and news functions of the media (e.g., Barnouw, 1978; Goldstein, 1985; Bagdikian, 1983). Advertising colors the way that entertainment and news programming convey information and ideas, determining how we understand and respond to health issues as individuals and as a society. "Network executives," Gitlin explains, "internalize the desires of advertisers as a whole" (1983, p. 253). This mindset results in the avoidance of controversy or any topic that might contaminate the fertile environment in which corporations seek to advertise their products.

The clearest example of the influence of advertisers over editorial content related to health issues can be seen in the tobacco industry. White and Whelan (1986) surveyed 20 American magazines in 1986 and found that magazines accepting cigarette advertising were much less likely to report on the hazards of smoking. They concluded that this underreporting was in large part due to self-censorship from fear of offending cigarette advertisers. In another review, Weis and Burke (1986) drew a similar conclusion.

Advertisers accept and promote the dominant theme of disease as individual flaw, thus reinforcing the view that the problem is in the person, not in the product. Responsibility for the consequences of decisions made by consumers reside not with the organizations that comprise the economic system but with the consumer.

In sum, advertising may well be a potent anti-health education force that serves to minimize the potential effects of health promotion campaigns. Advertising serves systematically to disassociate consumption from health risks and problems. It provides pervasive attractive messages that promote consumption, and through indirect economic pressure serves to limit the kind of health information Americans get through news and entertainment programming.

Reinforcement of Existing Social Arrangements

Historically, public health problems have always been linked to broader social and economic conditions. There is broad consensus in the field that health status is largely dependent on factors external to the individual over which he or she exercises little or no control (Mechanic, 1982). Health promotion, to be effective, is ultimately in the business of social change. The media, however, are in the business of preserving existing social arrangements. These conflicting goals lead to a dilemma in the use of mass media for meaningful health promotion. Health promotion, if it is to focus on the conditions that give rise to and sustain public health problems, will be extremely political and controversial. Moving the focus away from the individual and onto the broader environment is risky business. It leads to an emphasis on collective solutions to health problems, forces attention to reexamining basic values, and calls into question the wisdom of consumption as the primary driving social force.

The mass media seek to avoid controversy and maintain a good environment for consumption-oriented advertising. As might be expected, one of the primary messages from the mass media is allegiance to the social structure, not the need for fundamental changes in the system (Lazarsfeld & Merton, 1948). Early on, Lazarsfeld and Merton noted that mass media have a "narcoticizing effect" on the audience that lessens concern about social issues. Like Postman (1985), they argue that the flood of information contributes to passivity rather than action.

As Lazarsfeld and Merton explain, what is not said in the media may be more significant than what is said. In reinforcing the status quo, mass media generally ignore structural issues, "Hence by leading toward conformism and by providing little basis for a critical appraisal of society, the commercially sponsored mass media indirectly but effectively restrain the cogent development of a genuinely critical outlook" (1948, p. 503). It is this critical outlook that is essential to stimulate change and to create a foundation for addressing public health problems.

THE CHALLENGE

The challenge for the mass communication industries and the public health community is to make the greatest possible use of mass media to improve the health of the society. The problem emerges when it becomes clear that simply informing individuals about risk factors will not be sufficient to stimulate the type of change that is necessary to significantly improve health. One of the constraints within which we must plan and develop strategy is the simple reality that the goals of a corporate society are often in conflict with public health.

As the future role of the mass communication system in promoting the health of the public is discussed, it will be important to incorporate two key points. First, the positive role that mass media currently play should be identified and expanded. We have learned a great deal about the mass media as a positive social institution, and these lessons should be integrated. Second, there are new issues that must be addressed that have to do with overcoming the structural limitations of the mass communication system to respond to public health issues. These issues and their implications are sometimes difficult to define and often controversial to address.

(1) Mass media should continue to be used to set the public agenda and confer status and legitimacy on health issues. Public health professionals can work closely with media professionals to continue to keep health issues high on the public agenda. Drugs, AIDS, and heart disease are just three problems that have benefited from the collaboration of the health and communication professions.

(2) Public health and mass media professionals should continue to work together to communicate information to the citizenry regarding personal risk factors and approaches to addressing these risk factors. Although it may be the case that those most in need are not helped by public communication campaigns, it is important to continue to disseminate information through well-designed campaigns based on mass communication theories, social marketing principles, formative research methods, and community organization techniques. These campaigns will help some, probably those who are relatively better off, but will not be sufficient to stimulate significant change. Nonetheless, public communication campaigns are an important part of a comprehensive strategy of health promotion.

(3) Mass media professionals should continue to be responsive to efforts to insure the technical accuracy of facts related to health issues. The

"cooperative consultation" process developed by Breed and De Foe (1982) and related work by Backer (1988) provide a solid foundation for constructive relationships between entertainment media and health professionals.

(4) The greatest gains in health status will not come from changing individual behavior but from improvements in economic conditions and social justice across the society. The understanding of the social and economic generation of public health problems must receive a greater emphasis than individual level explanations. Public health professionals must work more closely with the mass media to communicate the root causes of disease and enhance popular understanding.

(5) Mass media professionals must be more willing to examine critically theories of disease causality and health promotion derived from the needs of a mass-production-oriented society. These theories lead us to question the motives and psychology of the individual who "abuses" a product but not the ethic of consumption that is skillfully promoted by marketers. The "manufacturers of illness" (McKinlay, 1979) should be singled out for attention at least as much as the individual casualties of the system.

(6) Finally, there is the larger issue of the role of mass media in a democratic society. Clearly, this role is to contribute to the development of knowledgeable people who are empowered and not disabled by the information they receive. People may not need increasing amounts of knowledge as much as they need skills for better analyzing and using knowledge.

If society is serious about promoting health, then the mass media must redefine the fundamental problem so that sufficiently broad strategies can be brought to bear. Even with the constraints of the mass media in contemporary society, there is potential for progress in this area. Mass media are too valuable a resource to be used as simple information and entertainment machines. They must be tools to enhance understanding.

This chapter has primarily emphasized the importance of television; given the saturation of this medium, the emphasis is appropriate. If mass media are to assume the leadership role in moving toward a healthier society, then it will be television that must lead the charge. Over 30 years ago Edward R. Murrow, speaking of television, explained: "This instrument can teach, it can illuminate; yes, and it can even inspire. But it can do so only to the extent that humans are determined to use it to those ends. Otherwise it is merely wires and lights in a box" (Murrow, 1958, p. 12).

Television, and the mass media in general, could make no greater contribution than to provide increased understanding that helps to build a safe, secure, and healthy society through improved social and economic conditions. It is these conditions that will truly form the basis for progressive public health strategies.

3

News Media Responsiveness to Public Health

PHILIP MEYER

News is conveyed through a manufacturing process. Constraints require information to be processed in a predictable, even ritualized, fashion so that it is gathered, evaluated, processed, and delivered on a continuous cycle. News people are forced to make quick judgments from imperfect information and deliver their product at a set time, ready or not.

WHAT IS NEWS?

The media do all of this in a competitive environment. There are no long-term contracts with readers or viewers, any of whom can switch to another medium or withdraw attention altogether. News is therefore processed and sold in a free market. It is not an efficient market in the sense that consumers know all the possible choices available to them and can always act rationally to further their own interests. But it is a market, and anyone wanting to use the news media to further a cause must first understand that market.

The textbook definitions of news include: *Timeliness* (news, by definition is new), *proximity* (especially geographical nearness), *consequence* (events that change or threaten to change people's lives), *human interest* (evoking an emotional response or illustrating a universal truth), *conflict* (the clash of opposing interests in war, sports or politics), *prominence* (e.g., the President), and *unusualness.*

52

These are the criteria by which newspeople consciously define news. But there are less visible constraints that also need to be understood by anyone who wants to be a part of the process.

Nontraditional Definitions

This second list is not found in textbooks:

Inoffensiveness. Editors protect the sensibilities of their readers, reminding each other that a newspaper is a family medium. This made it particularly difficult for writers to describe exactly how gay men transmit AIDS. David Shaw (1988) reports that the words "anal intercourse" did not appear in a newspaper until 1983.

The window of credibility. If an event is unusual (man bites dog), that helps it to qualify as news up to a point. Beyond that point, its unusualness creates such a strain on the belief system of the audience that it will not be attended to. In the late 1950s, glue sniffing was so bizarre that it was not pursued in the media. This is often the case with news that is too new. The window of credibility is narrow.

Fitting existing constructs. To avoid information overload, we perceive the world in terms of types and generalities—stereotypes. Collections of stereotypes form constructs or theoretical models through which we interpret the busy flow of facts and images. To qualify as news, an account must fit the prevailing constructs. Some sensitive social problems, such as racial discrimination, require efforts at deconstruction, but the cost to a news medium of attacking the prevailing constructs is high. One reason *The Washington Post* was alone on the Watergate story for so long was that to believe it required deconstruction of prevailing beliefs about the integrity of the people who governed us.

Packageable in daily bites. Competition and the daily cycle require news to be shaped into small, discrete packages, even when the events it describes may not be easily adaptable to that form. As James Reston (1967, pp. 194-195) has observed, "We are pretty good at reporting 'happenings,' particularly if they are dramatic. We are fascinated by events but not by the things that cause the events."

When the Surgeon General held a press conference to announce that the nicotine in tobacco is addictive, he received hostile questions from some reporters for telling them something that was not new. However, for the Surgeon General to say it in front of the cameras was new; an event was created that fit nicely into the smallest unit of broadcast news, the "sound bite" (technical jargon for a few seconds of intelligible spoken information). It is almost the electronic equivalent of a bumper sticker, and those who would use the media to advance their goals need to learn how to reduce their messages to sound bites and bumper stickers.

MEDIA WORLD VERSUS REAL WORLD

Information that meets the traditional and nontraditional tests of news value is not a representative sample of the universe of interesting and useful information. When people generalize from the picture of the world painted by the media to the real world, they are likely to be misled. Gerbner, Gross, Morgan, and Signorielli (1982) at the University of Pennsylvania have documented this situation for TV watchers; others have done it, specifically with respect to health issues, for newspaper readers.

For example, Combs and Slovic (1979) asked volunteer subjects to estimate death rates in the United States from a variety of causes. They also analyzed newspaper content to see what causes are written about most often. The researchers found that the causes of death reported in the press are a grossly distorted sample. More disturbing, the pictures in the heads of their subjects showed that personal assessments of risks reflected the spooky, violent world of newspaper content far more closely than they did the real world.

Freimuth, Greenberg, DeWitt, and Romano (1984) compared the frequency of newspaper mentions of types of cancer with their real-world incidence. Editors evidently think their readers will be offended by mention of colon or rectal cancer, which ranks seventh in coverage but first in incidence. Cancers of male and female reproductive organs get similar de-emphasis. Lung and breast cancer, on the other hand, are reported in rough proportion to their incidence.

Editors believe strongly that they have an affirmative duty to keep their audiences informed, even if there is no market demand for the information. In 1982, a representative sample of newspaper editors was asked this question: "Suppose that there were an issue that really meant a lot to the health and safety of people in your community, but people weren't very interested. Should the paper try to get people interested, or it should wait until their interest is aroused in some other way?"

Almost all editors replied that they should take the active stance and try to get interest aroused (Meyer, 1987). A similar response was found when the question was rephrased with specific issues in mind: the effect of seat belts in reducing traffic deaths, and the effect of diet on disease. However, these attitudes were not a good match to behavior. Even in 1988, few newspapers routinely report on the presence or absence of alcohol or seat belts as factors in stories about motor vehicle deaths. This lack of reporting may contribute to the public's longstanding underestimation of these risk factors.

Agenda-setting theory suggests that the media are capable of creating their own markets for information. If news values lead to distorted views of what is important in health care, the reading and viewing public will worry about the wrong things and demand more information about the wrong things. However, Culbertson and Stempel (1984) found that most people's personal health information agendas are set by their own specific problems rather than by national concerns raised by the media. This is both good and bad news. If the media distortions do not do measurable harm, then correcting them will do no measurable good.

EDITING AS A SOCIAL ACTIVITY

The definition of news also depends on factors beyond the events themselves. News definition depends on consensus.

Studies that cite the increasing concentration of media ownership as evidence of a decline in diversity of control over the news miss the mark. Uniformity in news judgments is caused not by ownership patterns but by a rigid system of social control that transcends organizational barriers. Editors have so many decisions to make, so many inputs and so little time to reflect, that they are understandably nervous about their own ability to judge the news. And so they watch each other. Small papers watch the wire service to decide what is important. At the top of this hierarchy of imitation stand *The New York Times* and *The Washington Post*, each of which watches the other. The *Times* is the dominant partner. It has been speculated that one reason the AIDS story took so long to gain national currency was the slow arousal of interest at the *Times*.

The same social pressures that keep editors from recognizing a phenomenon until their peers do also make them particularly susceptible to popular delusions and the madness of crowds. Genital herpes has been around at least since the days of the Roman emperor Tiberius, but few paid much attention to it until 1982 when it became the media disease of the year. Media accounts pushed the themes that incidence of the disease was growing to epidemic proportions, that it primarily afflicted the white middle class, and that it had devastating social, psychological and even physical consequences. A sober look back suggests that there is very little evidence that any of these themes was rooted in fact (Mirotznik & Mosellie, 1986). Other diseases of the moment—toxic shock syndrome in 1980 and Legionnaires disease in 1976—have been labeled "artificial outbreaks" based on media attention rather than anything happening in nature (Colburn, 1987).

PRESSURE FROM ADVERTISERS

Conspiracy theorists love advertisers. The theory that advertisers get not only ink and air time but control over the news for their money is at least straightforward. There is some anecdotal evidence of at least self-censorship on the part of editors to avoid offending advertisers. At least one case on record involves health news.

Paul Maccabee was the music editor of *Twin Cities Reader*, a weekly paper based in Minneapolis. He was sent to cover a jazz festival sponsored by Kool cigarettes. "Strange bedfellows, cigarettes and jazz," he wrote. "Duke Ellington died of lung cancer." The publisher who fired him said he was afraid of losing the four to five weekly pages of advertising bought by the cigarette industry.

Such control is not an economic imperative. An independent press is in the best interests of the advertisers because they need a credible medium to serve as a vehicle for their messages (the only ads in the supermarket tabloids are those addressed to people who will believe anything). An economically successful newspaper will prize its credibility more than the business of any single advertiser. It has plenty of other sources of revenue, while the advertisers most likely do not have equally good alternate outlets for their message. In the magazine industry, independence may be harder to obtain as increasing specialization limits the range of advertisers who support a publication.

EFFECTS OF COMPETITION

Competition keeps the media honest. It may indeed be its saving grace. The desire to be first with a story can give an editor or a reporter the backbone to go against the tide of the moment and report that a situation is black when everyone else is saying that it is white. But competition also has some undesirable effects.

News people compete with each other on an individual level that respects no patterns of ownership. Individuals in the same department of the same newspaper will fight to get priority for their stories, written the way they want them. The intensity of this competition creates an incentive to distort. Usually the distortion is benign. It consists of emphasizing the most outlandish or most alarming aspect of a situation in the lead and the backpedaling to provide perspective in the second or third paragraph. But in a world of sound bites and bumper stickers, the second or third paragraph may not be attended to.

Reynolds Packard wrote a novel called *The Kansas City Milkman* based on his experience as a foreign correspondent for United Press. In it he described the practice of inflating the number of people killed in a disaster because a wire editor, choosing between two versions of the same story, without any means of knowing which was true, would tend to prefer the inflated one. The next day, the service would report that the number of deaths was not as great as first estimated, thereby providing an angle with which to beat the competition again.

In making a story marketable, a reporter deals with tension between news value and credibility. If there is evidence that AIDS is being transmitted through heterosexual intercourse, that can meet the news values of consequence and timeliness. If the evidence is slim or heavily qualified, the qualification will get second billing. And it will not fit in the sound bite or on the bumper sticker. So the combined needs of competition and brevity often reduce news to near binary simplicity: AIDS is transmitted heterosexually; no it isn't. The most complicated medical stories get compressed into the binary categories of fear and hope.

That is why health journalism is biased toward two stock stereotypes: unrealistic fear of disease and other health hazards on the one hand; on the other, unrealistic belief in the magic of medicine. Over time, of course, the truth comes out. We are all eventually better informed from having attended to the media than if we had not.

SPECIALIZED REPORTING

The news business conditions its practitioners to a short attention span, yet adequately addressing complicated issues requires depth of treatment and attention. As a way around this problem, the media have created a category of journalists who have fewer things to think about and more time to think about them: specialists.

There are bright exceptions to the generally slow reaction time and superficial response of news media to the AIDS problem. In nearly every case, the reporters and editors who produced the insightful and detailed accounts were specialists in science and medicine coverage. It took their specialized knowledge to understand the situation and convey it to a lay audience.

Even such an obvious speciality as health and science writing has been slow to develop. Beat assignments in the newspaper business still tend to be casual. A reporter goes out on a beat because he or she is nearest at hand when the assignment is made. If successful, the reporter gets similar assignments, and a specialist is born.

As recently as 10 years ago, Sharon Dunwoody (1980) found that the science-writing community in this country is dominated by 25 to 30 veteran reporters. Investigators working for the National Cancer Institute reported that more than half of a sampling of 1980 news stories about cancer was written "by a small corps of science and medical reporters" (Freimuth et al., 1984). The fact that the corps is small is good news if the goal is to promote better-qualified specialists. It is easier to educate and persuade a small number of people than a large number. However, a larger number of health specialists in the media would create more diversity, leave more room for fresh viewpoints, and create a more efficient market for information by giving consumers a greater variety of choices.

BARRIERS IN THE HEALTH PROFESSIONS

The reward systems of organized science provide little benefit for communicating knowledge to the general public (Dunwoody & Ryan, 1984). In medicine, particularly, there are costs to publicity, because one's peers may see it as an unprofessional attempt at advertising or "self-aggrandizement." The concern is not ill founded. Naive journalists can be ready foils for scientists and health care providers who have narrow personal interests to advance.

The medical profession's response to problems of this sort is to try to control dissemination of new findings. The well-known policy of *The New England Journal of Medicine* to publish no finding that has appeared in the popular press is an example. Others feel that such a rigid policy comes at too high a cost. For knowledge to be advanced, a great variety of channels and audiences must be employed.

Scientists with experience in dealing with newsworthy research findings quickly perceive that building walls between themselves and the media is not a practical course. A better alternative is to set up channels of communication over which they can maintain some control. In its simplest form, the mechanism can be a list of experts in different specialties maintained by a professional society or public agency. The University of North Carolina at Chapel Hill, for example, publishes a volume called "experts on call" whom reporters are invited to call at any time at work or at home when they need specialized information.

Broadcasting especially needs this kind of help. The broader a medium's reach, the less specialized its reporters will usually be. People in the health sciences need a special effort to reach the nonexperts. Television talk shows have been singled out as a specially dangerous case. They have a built-in bias for charlatans because those without scientific substance for their claims have no other promotional route than the media. So they work hard to gain access to it. Whelan and Stanko (1983) have argued that the medical profession should fight back by being equally aggressive in seeking the media spotlight: "We cannot all be stars, but it would be worthwhile for physicians who appear frequently on the media to learn to present themselves and their messages with the proficiency of the average charlatan."

It seems apparent that educational efforts are needed at both ends. Health care professionals need to be better communicators, and journalists need to understand the subtleties of scientific method. A tall order, especially if there is no market for it. As long as the public wants its health information in sound bites and bumper stickers, progress will be limited.

4

Roles and Responsibilities of Journalists

STEPHEN KLAIDMAN

The principal imperatives that shape the 22 minutes of the network news programs or the 64 pages of a typical daily newspaper are well known. They are news judgment, which on any given day may be intelligent, incomprehensible, lemminglike, quirky, or some or all of the above; and the exigencies of audience share, which in print often means the triumph of writing over content and the selection of sexy stories over substantial ones, and on television frequently means pictures over all.

These imperatives, both of which embrace competitive considerations, generally apply to all areas of news coverage: politics and international affairs, business and economics, sports, entertainment, culture, etc. This is not surprising, for the American media are grounded in the ideals of an informed public and free enterprise. In the words of A. J. Liebling (1961, p. 7): "The function of the press in society is to inform, but its role is to make money."

The principal imperatives are not likely to change, and anyone who is concerned with the efficacy of informing the public about health would do well to avoid attacking the media on grounds of its fundamental approaches to news and commerce. Such an effort would almost certainly be fruitless, and it is also unnecessary because the media are beginning to seriously address the "litany of complaints" about the press coverage of science and health that Jay Winsten set out as follows:

That the press attributes an unjustified degree of certainty to new findings; that limited, incremental advances in research are portrayed inaccurately as major developments or breakthroughs; that the risks posed by putative health hazards are frequently exaggerated; that there often is a striking imbalance between the amount of attention accorded a piece of research and its actual scientific importance; that many medical news reports shamelessly exploit the emotions of desperately ill patients, their families, and the public at large; and that science news coverage often is plainly inaccurate due to errors of commission, omissions, or both. (Winsten, 1985, p. 6)

The media are responding by beginning to provide the kind of service-oriented coverage of health matters that a knowledgeable but disinterested observer would approve. This is most noticeable in the special health or science and health sections and programs that have proliferated in recent years. These include "Science Times" in *The New York Times* and its more recent weekly health pages; the "Health" section of *The Washington Post*, which is subtitled "A Weekly Journal of Medicine, Science and Society"; the weekly science page of the *Los Angeles Times*; the *Health Show* on ABC; and the regular segments on the network morning programs by physicians Art Ulene (NBC), Bob Arnot (CBS), and Timothy Johnson (ABC), who also appears frequently on the evening news and sometimes hosts *Nightline* when the subject has to do with medicine.

Moreover, major newspapers with news wires that service hundreds of other papers employ physicians as staff reporters. These fully trained professionals complement the increasing number of reporters who have some training in the biological sciences. This high quality coverage is available to medium-size and small newspapers in all regions of the country through the supplementary news services of the major dailies. This does not mean, of course, that editors will elect to use it. They will only do so if there is a perceived demand in the community.

Before proceeding to an analysis of the logic of news coverage, a distinction must be made between news and service coverage. News has been defined many different ways, but it must have been newly discovered, rediscovered, uncovered, or disclosed; it must involve something that a significant segment of the audience cares about; and it may be, but is not necessarily, controversial. One of the things that sets these new health sections and programs apart from the rest of the news vehicle is that much of what they report is not news as traditionally defined. It is instead an effort to satisfy the ongoing needs and desires of readers and viewers for information related to personal health and other aspects of the health care enterprise that concern them.

The significance of the distinction is that in a service section the traditional news imperatives lose much of their relevance. Competition is still important, but since the sections are more carefully designed to serve the perceived needs of the audience than traditional news coverage, the competition is to see who can most accurately perceive and most effectively serve these needs. The articles need not be newsy, although they might well be trendy. The emphasis is not on publishing or broadcasting something first, but rather on reporting it in an understandable, accurate, informative, substantially complete, and useful fashion. It is also noteworthy that these sections and programs have a spillover effect into food and lifestyle sections and programs, which are carrying more and more health-related information.

The increase in the number of health sections and programs does not indicate a new interest in health coverage on the part of mass media, although interest does appear to be increasing. A recent study by Hill and Knowlton (DeVries, 1988) showing that "40% of all stories in daily newspapers are health-related" is not significantly out of line with earlier research.

A partial rundown of the table of contents of a typical issue of "Health," which appears each Tuesday in *The Washington Post*, provides a sense of what is meant by service-oriented articles. For example, the lead article of the June 14, 1988, issue, titled "Risk vs. Reality," explains the difference between the scientist's view of risk and the public's view of risk; "Fussy Babies" deals with whether the traits of infancy persist into adulthood; "The Patient's Advocate," a regular feature, discusses a proposal to organize medical knowledge for the benefit of both patients and physicians; and another regular feature, "Consultant," which is written by a physician, answers readers' medical questions.

None of this is traditional news fare. It is, however, the kind of information health professionals are eager to communicate to the public. Moreover, these sections and programs are often open to contributions from professionals who are unaffiliated with the newspaper or network and have insights to share or information to impart. There are no comprehensive data available on the use of service-oriented health stories by the roughly 1,700 daily newspapers around the country, but according to editors at *The New York Times* News Service, virtually all of their health coverage goes out on the wire to their 330 domestic clients. Editors at the *Los Angeles Times-Washington Post* News Service say that about 75% of what they publish in the "Health" section goes out to about 350 client papers in the United States and Canada.

THE LOGIC OF NEWS IN HEALTH REPORTING

Aside from the specialized health information vehicles, much of the mass media coverage of health involves traditional news reporting, which operates under the overarching logic of "news." This section examines several sublogics that play a significant role in determining coverage.

The Affected

AIDS has demonstrated better than any health story in recent memory that unless the mass media's core middle-class constituency is perceived to be at risk, a disease does not constitute a story. AIDS was initially perceived as affecting homosexuals, hemophiliacs, and Haitians, and it was thought to be spread chiefly by sexual practices deemed unfit for polite discourse in general-circulation newspapers or on the broadcast media. J. Ronald Milavsky (1988) quoted Professor Herbert Gans as saying that news may "involve a large number of people, especially 'our kind of people.'" Editors and reporters are overwhelmingly white, middle-class, and heterosexual. Milavsky goes on to say that "news decisionmakers are guided [inter alia] by assumptions about the needs, interests and values of the audience, [and that] most mass media try to attract and maintain the broad middle of the social landscape by keeping a mainstream tone and avoiding things that might drive audiences away—like bad taste" (p. 6). These assumptions presumably contributed to the fact that "it took the [New York] *Times*, which is published in the city that accounted for more than half of all known cases at that time—a thousand AIDS cases—three years to give the epidemic prominent coverage" (Milavsky, 1988, p. 7).

Other diseases that affect limited populations, such as sickle-cell anemia and Tay-Sachs disease, are covered, but in a very limited fashion and often because there is a human-interest component relating to suffering per se as opposed to health-related considerations. Major killers that are not identified with a discrete population such as heart disease, cancer, stroke, and accidents (including automobile) tend to be covered whenever there is a "news peg."

In the case of AIDS it is clear that the media collectively made a mistake. The significance of the epidemic was not appreciated as early as it might have been, and therefore the quantity and depth of coverage were inadequate. When certain events came to light, such as cases involving children in school and Rock Hudson's announcement that he had AIDS, media attention increased dramatically. It took even more time before that attention was directed to important issues of policy and funding, but eventually that also came.

Could anyone have done anything to focus the media's attention sooner? The answer is almost certainly yes, but those who were best placed to do it were federal officials working for an administration that was not initially disposed to do much about AIDS for economic and moralistic reasons. A president can move the media on any subject. All he need do is address it, something President Reagan chose not to do on AIDS until late in his second term. Close personal relationships with editors can also be enormously important. If, for example, an AIDS medical specialist had been a trusted friend of A. M. Rosenthal, executive editor of *The New York Times* during the first five years of the epidemic, that could have made a major difference. If Rosenthal (i.e., the *Times*) had recognized the importance of AIDS earlier, everyone else would have followed, for the *Times* is an agenda-setter for both print and electronic media.

If a disease, as was the case of AIDS, is perceived as affecting "them" and not "us," it will inevitably get less media coverage than if it is seen as a threat to everyone, or to "us" and not "them." If that perception cannot be changed, or if it cannot be demonstrated to the satisfaction of editors that it is truly likely to devastate the community it threatens, then the mass media are not likely to be interested in providing extensive coverage.

Investigative Journalism

The ruling logic of the investigative journalist is to accumulate in exquisite detail the evidence required to support a strongly held hypothesis. When the hypothesis is correct, it can be a marvelously effective way of bringing the public's attention to injustice (as in nursing home scandals), bad science (as in stories involving falsified and invented experiments), and health-related social problems (such as patient dumping). The problem with this system of journalistic inquiry is that it often leads to both conscious and subconscious rejection of evidence that is at odds with the hypothesis. In the field of health reporting this can damage the reputations of physicians and scientists, the relationship between physicians and their patients, and the confidence of patients in beneficial forms of treatment. One specific case where all of these things happened is instructive: a series of articles on the "War on Cancer" that appeared in *The Washington Post* (Klaidman & Beauchamp, 1987).

In 1981, the *Post* ran front page stories over four consecutive days. The subtitle of the lead-off series was "First Do No Harm." The reporters assigned to the project were Ted Gup and Jonathan Neumann, both young members of the Metropolitan staff with no special training in science or medicine. They both had a bent for investigative reporting, and they were given the freedom to determine precisely which aspect of the battle against cancer they would pursue. They were also given an extraordinary amount of time to complete their project.

Gup and Neumann elected to investigate the experimental drug program of the National Cancer Institute and even more specifically, Phase One drug trials, which are intended to determine the toxicity of experimental drugs and the dose response of terminally ill patients. The hypothesis was that there were significant and documentable problems with the experimental program. Gup and Neumann set out to find them. After their year of reporting, they wrote that unwitting patients were being given experimental drugs with a primary purpose that was not therapeutic; that hundreds of patients had died as a result of the drugs they were given; and that many others had suffered severe side-effects. The overall thrust of the series was that patients were being duped into taking drugs that could do them no good, although others might eventually be helped by them, and that in some cases patients were being fraudulently led to believe that these drugs were their last hope for recovery.

Gup and Neumann chronicled case after case in which they emphasized that experimental drugs were linked to the deaths of cancer patients. They placed far less emphasis on the fact that all of these patients were terminally ill. They chronicled these often heartbreaking horror stories in 450 column inches over four days, and accompanied them with two brief success stories, and an excerpt from an interview with Dr. Vincent DeVita, head of NCI, and some comments on and criticisms of the series by DeVita.

The series was deeply flawed in several ways. First, it left the inaccurate impression that the Phase One trials were run by a set of coldly efficient scientists who were conducting inhuman experiments on unwitting patients who had been fraudulently led to believe that there was more than a minuscule chance that experimental drug treatment would significantly extend their lives. Second, it blurred the distinction between experimental therapies and clinically approved chemotherapy. Third, it failed to make the point that anti-cancer drugs must be toxic to work and that testing for levels of toxicity is an absolutely necessary part of the process of developing effective drugs. Fourth, they sensationalized bizarre-sounding irrelevancies, such as the fact that one drug contained a dye used in ballpoint pen ink. Fifth, they did not take note of the important fact that cancer is tens or even hundreds of diseases and that a drug that might fail against one type of cancer could well succeed against another. Sixth, they ignored the concept that anti-cancer drugs are meant to be combined with surgical and radiation treatment and that drugs are expected to be most effective in treating early rather than advanced cancers. Finally, the series said that only six experimental drugs had proved effective against cancer. According to NCI, the correct number at the time was 49.

The negative cast of the series, its many flaws, and the extraordinary display it was given combined to frighten patients and enrage physicians. Moreover, the fact that the *Post* was severely and justifiably criticized for the series, both in the Washington community and in the journalism community, put an end to the larger and potentially valuable project on the fight against cancer in America. The *Post* was there because of a hypothesis that something was wrong. A series that said all is well at the NCI would not have justified the extraordinary investment in time. The *Post*'s cancer series was an example of the logic of investigative reporting gone beserk. More commonly, the damage is more limited, but for those involved just as harmful. In the long run, there is no perfect solution, but the education and sensitization of journalists about the methods and matter of science and medicine will help.

Hard Choices and New Technology

Ethical dilemmas and technological developments are two inter-twined areas that the media find irresistible. In the somewhat cynical view of heart transplant surgeon Christiaan N. Barnard (1973, p. 121), "Spare-part surgery provided a windfall of copy and 'comment' to fill the spaces between the advertisements and commercials that make the whole mass communication enterprise viable in the first place." Be-cause of the development of sophisticated new medical technologies, it is possible to extend life, to begin it in glass dishes, and to modify it. Because of the drama inherent in these life-and-death decisions, and because they involve fundamental moral questions, they will continue to command the interest of the media and the public.

The case of Baby Jane Doe, which took place on Long Island in the metropolitan New York area, is interesting because *The New York Times* was outperformed, as was everyone else, by a suburban paper— *Newsday*.

The principal controversy was over whether a child born with spina bifida and microcephaly should be kept alive. As it developed the case involved medical, legal, political, social, and philosophical issues. And obviously, from start to finish, it was high in human-interest content. Although it received substantial coverage in the major media, it was not well covered.

Most of the articles in the print press were written with the implica-tion that the facts were known and that Baby Jane Doe's future, if she were to live, would be extremely grim. By contrast, a sampling of medical opinion at the time suggested that the prognosis was not nearly as predictable or grim as a sampling of the national press would have indicated. An accurate report at the time would have broken a journal-istic convention by focusing on uncertainty as the central knowable truth. As for television, the anguish of the infant's parents was made for the medium. Under television lights, the logic of human interest grows by orders of magnitude.

But *Newsday* mastered the story in print with an impressive effort led by reporters Kathleen Kerr and B. D. Colen. It did so by answering questions regarding consensus in the medical community about how to treat Baby Jane Doe's constellation of conditions, the child's potential quality of life, the legal basis for government intervention, the real basis for the parents' original decision to forgo life-lengthening surgery, and the implications of this case for other cases involving handicapped infants, children, or adults (Klaidman & Beauchamp, 1986).

OTHER LOGICS

There are many other news logics such as heroes and villains and the personal concerns and habits of editors and publishers, but two deserve special mention: fads and economics.

A fad is something in which a lot of people are intensely interested, so they will read about it or watch television news items about it. Health fads range from acupuncture to rolfing; the ones that are currently most popular have to do with diet and exercise. Health fads may be genuinely beneficial, harmless, or harmful. Stories about them written by skilled reporters will generally provide the information needed to determine how they should be approached. The risks and benefits will be spelled out so that they can be understood by readers. Warnings will be issued about serious dangers. And some effort will be made to reconcile apparently contradictory, or confusing scientific findings such as those indicating that there is good cholesterol and bad cholesterol, good fat and bad fat.

Stories about health fads will turn up regularly in the service sections and on the special health segments and programs on television, but when they are new and when there are new developments related to them, they appear in the news sections and are subject to the other logics of news (e.g., human interest: irony in the death while running of James Fixx, who helped to popularize running for exercise).

The logic of economics is best illustrated by the well-known history of news coverage of smoking (Taylor, 1984; White, 1988). Despite the best intentions of editors, the influence of advertisers can creep into the newsroom, more easily but not exclusively in financially weak news organizations. It takes a continuous effort on the part of journalists and citizens to overcome an unholy alliance between publishers and advertisers, but, as the smoking case demonstrates, at a certain point the combination of public pressure and the weight of the evidence can conspire to bring about change.

There is a second logic of economics. If there is a lot of money involved, an event becomes a story. This is true, for example, of questions involving health insurance, malpractice verdicts, and insurance rates. When a $10 million dollar verdict is rendered against obstetricians who carry $4 million worth of insurance, that is news, as is the fact that the average annual malpractice premium for obstetricians in Florida is $153,000. For the most part this kind of coverage serves the generally desirable purpose of keeping citizens informed about important health-related matters in their communities. However, such coverage may be flawed if, for example, a malpractice case is complicated and reporters are unable to assess the conflicting testimony of expert witnesses.

A PRESCRIPTION FOR HEALTH NEWS

The governing perspective of this chapter has been the requirements of a consumer of health information who is reasonably intelligent and always rational. This hypothetical reader or viewer provides a standard for the presentation of health-related information. Such a person is interested in substantially complete, understandable, accurate, relatively objective, relevant information about health risks, policy, costs, and scientific developments (Klaidman & Beauchamp, 1987). This consumer also cares about mistakes, fraud, charlatanism, bad science, price gouging, misappropriation of funds, bad research choices, and anything else going on in the health sphere that should not be. The two categories overlap one another, and they fall into the purviews of both service sections and news pages, special health programs and the nightly news.

In our democracy, citizens consider it to be in the public interest and in the interest of the entire health care enterprise that information on these matters be made available. With that as a given, there is no current alternative to mass media as the principal distribution network. Therefore, it is desirable that health professionals cooperate with the media in a prudent fashion and with the public interest in mind. There is, of course, no clear consensus among health professionals as to what constitutes prudence or the public interest in the diverse circumstances of providing health-related information to a public of widely varied sophistication. Moreover, the imperatives of science and medicine are often inconsistent with the imperatives of journalism.

What can be done to overcome these obstacles to useful coverage of health matters? First, do not waste time or effort on trying to change the basic culture of the news business. A challenging, long-term task that in the end might prove more fruitful would be to work toward improving the general level of public knowledge about health science and other health-related matters, thereby creating greater public demand for more thoughtful coverage. An increase in the number of programs devoted to training journalists in health reporting is desirable, as is an increase in communications programs for scientists. Another distant goal worth pursuing is the education of editors. Health and science reporters are complaining less about scientists and physicians these days and more about their editors. In this sphere, the most encouraging sign is the advent of the health sections, which often are run by trained, committed editors.

None of this, of course, will come easy, nor will it produce dramatic change. Among other things, old attitudes die hard and physicians and journalists will continue to approach each other warily. For many physicians, the words of Sir William Osler still ring true:

> In the life of every successful physician there comes the temptation to toy with the Delilah of the press—daily and otherwise. There are times when she may be courted with satisfaction, but beware! Sooner or later she is sure to play the harlot, and has left many a man shorn of his strength, viz. the confidence of his professional brethren. (Osler, 1905, p. 69)

Suffice to say that on the journalism side of the divide there are those whose view of physicians is no more flattering than Sir William's view of journalists.

5

Public Health and the Media:
Unequal Partners?

STEPHEN C. STUYCK

A discussion about how the public health community responds to the mass media must begin by acknowledging the diversity that characterizes institutions, disciplines, and individuals within the fields of health care delivery, biomedical science, and public health promotion. The purposes and constituencies of those organizations differ, and so do their marketing goals. More than any other single factor, those differences will influence the approach to working with the media and account for much of the harmony, or lack of harmony, that the institution enjoys in the relationship. The media-related issues for a public health agency implementing a disease-prevention program are quite different from the issues that confront a research institution attempting to interpret complex and obscure scientific advances under the pressures of hard-news deadlines. Several categories of factors tend to affect the public health community's responsiveness to the mass media.

CONFLICTING INTERESTS

Reduced to simplest terms, the public health community usually looks to the media for support, for attention, and for endorsement—for positive coverage. The media, in turn, seek "news" that is interesting and relevant to their audiences. The definition of what is "news" may frequently be in debate, but it is always determined by the media themselves. Many in the public health community have a hard time understanding how the media make choices about news coverage, and to many persons in the scientific community, it appears that "news" and "bad news" often are synonymous. Those in the complex areas of public health and biomedical science seek from the media an understanding of "shades of gray" in a media environment that encourages and rewards "black and white." The public health community likes qualifying adjectives, detailed explanations, and disclaimers that may actually reduce what an editor might view as the news "value" of a story.

UNEQUAL RELATIONSHIP

The public health community needs the media more than the media need the public health community. This lopsided relationship can cause disappointment, especially as more persons in the public health community (some without much media sophistication) come to depend on mass media to support their efforts in health education and develop expectations of the media that cannot always be met.

Newness adds to the uneasiness about the balance in this relationship. It was not very long ago that many in the biomedical community were relatively indifferent to working with the media. Two sets of factors have dramatically changed all that. One is the wave of interest in healthy living, based upon the growing body of scientific data that provide the foundation for disease prevention and risk reduction programs. Health educators have programs to sell and important messages to convey and, fortunately, the media are responsive and should take great credit for helping to stimulate that movement.

A second factor concerns the trends in medical practice, consumerism, reimbursement, declining lengths of hospital stays, and the like that are causing fundamental, irrevocable change in health care delivery in the United States. Those changes make the health community more dependent on the media to enhance the consumer's knowledge about the options that are now available in an incredibly competitive marketplace. Media coverage of a medical center can provide the visibility and credibility that paid advertising cannot guarantee, at least at a level most organizations in the public health sector can afford to buy.

COMPETITION

Public health specialists and agencies are competing more aggressively for a larger share of the media pie. Media time and space are finite, so agencies will "compete" with other agencies, causes with other causes, and the strong will survive.

Most health care news is "soft" by media standards and can be covered or ignored without any serious, immediate ramifications. The marginal nature of health news can lead to lost opportunities, especially if the person serving as intermediary between the "message" and the media is not particularly effective. Robert Bazell, the science and health correspondent for NBC News, has criticized two types of public relations officers: the one who thinks that everything going on is important and the one who thinks that nothing going on is important. "Both are equal sins," Bazell says. "The *latter* is more common."

Competition also is leading to something very positive: creativity. The good productive tension generated by competition is causing the public health community to think in new ways and create new methods of communication that cater to media needs—direct electronic links to news rooms, video news releases, and gratis B-roll, an entire cottage industry that has developed in writing op-ed pieces, and many more.

MESSAGE CONTROL

Public health agencies often have unrealistic expectations about message control. Those in the public health sector may often assume they have far greater control over the format and content of the health message that is sent to the intended audience than they actually do.

On the part of the public health community, there can be a tremendous investment of time, energy, and funds in the development of media communication tools. Despite good intentions, and often because of a lack of expertise, sometimes things do not go as they were conceived. This can manifest itself in several ways: public service announcements that air at odd hours or too infrequently for real impact, newspaper stories that "deserved" better play, and interviews that take place but never see the light of day.

For television, the special constraints of short air time, long set-up time, and the need to visualize a story have a lot to do with message control, especially in a field like cancer. However, television has introduced positive programming changes in its approach to covering health (coverage of single subjects on ABC-TV's *Nightline* is a good example), so probably more is made of the "special constraints" of television than those constraints really merit.

If the public health sector is to succeed in developing messages that are used (and used relatively intact), then the messages must be packaged in terms that are appealing to media format and relevant to media needs per se, as well as to the needs of the intended audience.

ERRORS OF FACT AND INTERPRETATION

Factual errors can be trivial or of great consequence, but they all cause some headaches and chip away at the confidence of the public health community in the mass media. From the public health perspective, those mistakes occur more frequently than the media appear to acknowledge, and there is relatively little recourse for correction.

A greater problem is the error that results from interpretation, and both parties share the responsibility for this. Journalists sometimes misunderstand, sometimes have ideas that are not accurate, and sometimes try too hard to make stories "relevant."

Scientists sometimes talk too obscurely, misstate the facts, or regret their *accurately* reported words once they hear or read them. But there is also a need for scientists and physicians who have a greater understanding of the priorities of the media and a willingness to meet reporters half-way.

With some work, the media and their sources might do more to form the "shared culture" that emphasizes cooperation rather than conflict, something that largely does not exist at present, except for a small circle of elite science journalists. While a "shared culture" would be inappropriate in the realm of "hard" news, it could contribute toward more informative media coverage in areas such as wellness, disease prevention and risk reduction, which are mainly considered "soft" news.

OPPORTUNITIES

Several years ago, M. D. Anderson Cancer Center undertook a study of 437 mass-media gatekeepers in Texas designed to determine the existing and potential roles of mass media in cancer education and information. The study examined gatekeepers' beliefs concerning the major health problems facing society, their perceptions of their roles within their organizations, and their opinions concerning the factors that influence their decisions about news coverage, usefulness of the cancer information they receive, and practices concerning coverage of cancer news. The goal was to identify ways in which the public health community might rethink its approach to media relations by looking at that relationship through the eyes of the media. The responses of gatekeepers suggest the following key recommendations for health educators.

Knowledge: Be Armed with Information
Before Approaching the Media

The gatekeepers acknowledge "public education" as a responsibility of the news media, but they expect the public health community to be informed about the issues at hand and about the news media's needs.

Impact: Disease Morbidity and Mortality per se
Will Not Guarantee Media Interest

The research showed that media gatekeepers consider cancer to be a far greater health problem than cardiovascular disease, for example, despite the fact that each year heart disease kills more than twice as many Americans as cancer does. Among respondents, there was little correlation between the prevalence or impact of a host of diseases or problems and their relative rank among health issues. This suggests that the public health community may need to educate gatekeepers before they can expect media interest or support. It also may mean that those from the public health sector who approach the media with the best information and most persuasive arguments may be most successful in generating media interest.

Visibility: Be Aggressive, But Have Something to Say

Many mass media stories are "pitched" to the media by a source. The survey confirmed that media acknowledge a direct connection between contacts by the public health community and action on their part. The gatekeepers rated their own expertise or interest of little consequence in covering a story, which demonstrates the vital educational role that the public health community can play with the media.

Independence: What Other Media
Do Does Not Appear to Matter

The gatekeepers did not identify "the actions of other media" as an important factor in their decisions to cover cancer news. While this could reflect a denial that media sometimes follow the lead of other media or the survey's focus on soft-news subject matter, it appears that health educators must make their own case rather than rely on what has been done by other media in order to convince gatekeepers.

Credibility: Media Pay More Attention to
Information from Credible Sources

The media are more likely to cover a story from sources they perceive as "credible." This is heartening news for those who represent institutions that are part of the medical "establishment." The reputation of the news source was rated significantly higher than other factors when determining which news to print or broadcast.

Consumerism: Media Want Information They Consider Useful

Gatekeepers expressed great interest in helping their audiences become informed consumers on health matters. As expected, media professionals expressed wariness about information they deemed "promotional" in nature and were most interested in information that they thought would benefit their audience. Herein lies the greatest source of encouragement for those in the public health community with messages about prevention, risk reduction, new treatment options, and the like.

Clarity/Brevity: The Greatest Challenge to the
Public Health Community

Gatekeepers want health information materials that are concise and clear, largely for reasons of space and time limitations. More than 60% said they did not use health information they receive, either because the "format was inappropriate" or because it was "uninteresting." We found great interest among gatekeepers in receiving materials that they perceive as relevant to their audiences and of help in doing their jobs.

CONCLUSION

"Partnership" or not, it is apparent that most of the responsibility for further enhancing the relationship between the mass media and the public health community rests with those in public health. Media agendas are set by a host of economic and political forces, with health but one of the subjects deemed by gatekeepers to be relevant to audiences. Because mass media acknowledge their important role in public education, the task remains to make health information understandable, compelling, and easily accessible. In doing so, the public health community can accomplish two goals: reach people with vital information, and help the media fulfill their self-described mission.

6

Controversies in Advertising of Health-Related Products

WILLIAM NOVELLI

In modern America, the mass media are basically channels of commerce. Public relations and advertising are combined with trade and consumer promotion, direct marketing, and personal selling to achieve sales, revenue, and profit goals. Two of these disciplines, advertising and public relations, are most often implemented through mass media channels. To communicate sales messages, advertisers purchase time and space in media, including television, radio, newspapers, magazines, transit vehicles, and billboards.

Public relations practitioners have a different approach to using the media. Rather than purchasing time or space, they must persuade media "gatekeepers" to carry their information. These gatekeepers include writers, producers, editors, talk show coordinators, and newscasters. As a result of such media placements, the public relations message finds its way into news and feature stories, editorials, op-ed pieces, news and talk show appearances, entertainment reviews, syndicated columns, and television programs.

Among the commercial messages, some offer "health" products (e.g., vitamins, headache remedies, running shoes). Others use health and nutrition claims and imagery to promote any manner of goods and

AUTHOR'S NOTE: I would like to thank Ellen Eisner and Dr. Theresa Marron-Grodsky for their assistance in researching and preparing this chapter.

services (e.g., snack foods, cereal, mattresses, fruit juice, retirement communities, vacation resorts, and cosmetics). Still other marketing communication efforts encourage unhealthful behaviors (e.g., smoking, fast driving). The common characteristic among all these commercial efforts is that goods and services are being sold in a profit-making endeavor. The message claims, promises, images, and effects are part of the sell.

Wallack presents a negative view of commercial messages in the American marketplace (see Chapter 2). He asserts that these messages promote higher levels of potentially health-compromising products through life-style appeals, and that they often contain product information that is either irrelevant to the consumer or misleading and deceptive.

In addition to these negatives, perhaps the most enduring criticism is that advertising and other marketing communications manipulate consumers by creating (possibly unnecessary) wants rather than satisfying needs.

On the positive side, it may be argued that commercial enterprise via the media is subject to regulation, has improved America's standard of living (and thus helped improve the nation's health status), makes affordable and possible (via taxes, contributions, public service, and in other ways) public-sector efforts in health promotion and disease prevention, and provides useful information (enabling free choice without coercion).

This chapter focuses on several controversial issues in the promotion of health-related products, beginning with an examination of various claims in commercial messages for foods. This is followed by a description of problems associated with advertising of three sensitive product categories: alcohol, cigarettes, and pharmaceuticals. The closing sections discuss avenues of cooperation between commercial and public health sectors (illustrated by the collaboration between Kellogg's and the National Cancer Institute) and the concept of social responsibility in marketing.

HEALTH AND NUTRITION CLAIMS

In discussing commercial messages that relate to health, it is useful to distinguish between a health claim and a nutrition claim. A health claim makes a specific link between use of the product being promoted and some health benefit. A nutrition claim makes statements about the nutrient content of foods, but it does not suggest anything about expected health benefits from using the product.

Since 1984, the Federal Trade Commission has encouraged food producers to make health claims in their marketing campaigns as a way of communicating more health-related information to the consumer.

Most health claims are not unique to a particular product, and therefore, there is little opportunity for marketers to differentiate their brands from competitors in the same category. John Stanton, professor of food marketing at St. Joseph's University in Pennsylvania, believes that this lack of ability for brand differentiation is a serious detriment to the greater use of health claims by marketing companies (Stanton, 1987). But he foresees increased use of such claims by trade associations to boost the image of commodity foods (e.g., orange juice, dates, table grapes) rather than to sell individual brands.

Another possible restraint on health claims is the increasing interest of state officials in investigating false and misleading claims (e.g., promoting bean and pea soups as high-fiber sources).

Finally, health and nutrition claims may be affected by the anticipated decline of the "age of deregulation." Howard Bell, President of the American Advertising Federation, believes that the next period will be one of revived and increased consumer activism, with corresponding industry retrenchment and increased self-regulation. Congress may be persuaded to intervene in the belief that regulatory agencies are not sufficiently active (AAF, 1988).

MISLEADING HEALTH-RELATED CLAIMS

In attempting to gain an edge over competition and/or to capitalize on consumer health interests and trends, marketing communicators can make statements that may confuse or mislead the public. For example, Campbell Soup advertising suggested that soups may help reduce the risk of cancer and are a good source of calcium. Critics pointed out that the calcium comes largely from the milk that the consumer adds in preparing the soup. Moreover, critics contended that the product has high sodium levels, which were not disclosed, and which made health claims inappropriate.

Also, Quaker Oats implied that eating oatmeal or oat bran could reduce cholesterol levels by 10%. The Center for Science in the Public Interest (CSPI) claimed that Quaker's own data indicated that oats might reduce cholesterol levels by approximately 3%.

In some cases, a claim may be inaccurate (the Quaker Oats cholesterol level statement). Another problem may be that the message may state information accurately, but not address other product attributes that are "negative" (nondisclosure of high sodium levels by Campbell Soup). Industry spokespersons argue that companies can hardly be expected to list negative product attributes, unless required to by law.

Industry self-regulation, government regulation, and the monitoring of consumer groups are checks and balances to product and service claims. In the intensely competitive climate of the American marketplace, companies will continue to push for unique, believable, and important selling promises that give them an edge.

PROBLEMS WITH ALCOHOL PRODUCTS

Beer and wine are among the most heavily advertised product categories on television and radio. Liquor advertising (not presently seen in broadcast media because of voluntary restrictions) is a major source of revenue for magazines and, to a lesser degree, newspapers. Beer promotion and consumption are so interwoven with the economics and social patterns of American sports that it might be difficult for many major and minor sports to survive in their current form without the revenues from this product.

Critics charge that marketers of alcoholic beverage products clearly focus on heavy drinkers. As evidence, they point to ads purchased by magazines in trade journals to convince alcohol producers that their periodicals reach readers who consume alcohol heavily.

Another complaint leveled at alcoholic beverage advertising is that some campaigns encourage greater consumption and suggest that alcohol is an appropriate mechanism for coping with personal problems. For instance, Southern Comfort is said to appeal to the need for relief, comfort, and escape. Crown Royal will help the troubled "get it all together."

Intense criticism is aimed at purported efforts by companies to target entry-level drinkers. Atkin and Block (1980) report that, compared to adult respondents, adolescents report higher exposure to alcoholic beverage advertising, are more impressed with endorsements by celebrities, and are more likely to say they will consume the advertised beverage.

College campuses are well-defined markets, and various product promotions for alcoholic beverages are integrated into campus life. It is estimated that about $10 million is invested in college newspapers annually in alcohol advertising. The increased drinking ages in most states have apparently not affected placements of ads in student newspapers. Critics say that it is difficult to claim that such an audience belongs to an existing drinker market when many are underage and others are barely of legal age.

Another area of criticism relates to the audience composition of television programming. Audiences are so diverse that children, adolescents, and adults may all watch a single sporting event or other program. Critics claim that widespread beer and wine (including wine cooler) advertising in the medium contributes to the impression that drinking is a healthful activity and a normal part of growing up.

The overwhelming majority of Americans who consume alcoholic beverages do so in moderation. At the same time, the health, social and economic costs of alcohol problems is great, totaling approximately $117 billion and 100,000 lives annually. The responsible marketing of these products is an issue as complex and important as the related issue of responsible consumption.

MARKETING COMMUNICATIONS AND CIGARETTES

The health hazards attributed to tobacco products are now well-known, but a generation ago health claims were used as part of the communications efforts. For example, Lucky Strike was positioned as an aid to weight loss ("Reach for a Lucky Instead of a Sweet"). In advertising for L&M, movie stars such as Rosalind Russell and Barbara Stanwyck proclaimed, "L&M's filters are just what the doctor ordered."

As more became known about the health consequences of smoking, the advertising of cigarette brands came under more regulation. For the past two decades, cigarette advertising has been banned from television and radio.

Print advertising has continued, however, and promotion and public relations expenditures have been heavy. Sponsorships of jazz and country music festivals, automobile racing, tennis, and other events have kept brand recognition high. Signage at sports stadia and arenas, ads in sports programs, funding for the arts, ethnic programs, and other means of communication have served to promote smoking products.

Despite numerous legislative initiatives, no changes appear imminent in the regulations now governing cigarette advertising and promotion. However, as social norms swing away from smoking as acceptable behavior, the cigarette companies themselves are rethinking their communication strategies. For example, less visible approaches (such as direct mail) are likely to grow as a result of improved computer database management, and as general awareness about cigarette promotion becomes less desirable to tobacco companies.

A major concern of antismoking advocates is that tobacco companies apparently are seeking to protect their markets during declining consumption by aggressively targeting minorities, youth, and women. As smoking continues to decline, it may eventually be most common among Americans of lower social-economic status. This will make it more difficult to reach smokers with effective prevention and cessation messages. As with many health problems in the United States, health-threatening behavior is often most resistant to change among "downscale" consumers.

DIRECT-TO-CONSUMER PHARMACEUTICAL ADVERTISING

Public relations activities (e.g., placing a physician spokesperson on a TV talk show) are commonly used to communicate awareness about ethical drugs to consumers. This is done in combination with advertising and promotion to health professionals. The overall purpose is to create a "pull" strategy (consumer demand) to work in concert with a "push" strategy (through the health professional channels).

In recent years, a new approach has been added to the communications mix. No issue in pharmaceutical marketing is currently attracting as much attention as direct-to-consumer (DTC) advertising of ethical drugs (e.g., the "Partners in Healthcare" campaign by Pfizer on the physician-patient relationship and early screening, and Squibb's "Quality of Life" advertising campaign for Capoten). Some see this as the wave of the future, but questions about its effectiveness, as well as the FDA's uneasiness about the practice, may limit its use.

From a consumer perspective, there are several factors for and against the use of DTC advertising. DTC advertising meets consumers' desire for health care information; aspects of such advertising can inform the public about health issues apart from providing drug-specific claims; and DTC advertising can provide information about less expensive alternatives.

On the negative side, such advertising might negatively influence the physician-patient relationship, and consumers may be frightened and confused by prescribing information and/or the "fair balance" statement that must accompany product-specific ads.

From a commercial marketing perspective there are also both positive and negative considerations to DTC advertising. Factors that pharmaceutical companies may find in favor of such an approach include the presently uncrowded consumer advertising landscape (only a few pharmaceutical companies now produce DTC ads), the ability to communicate a unique product feature that can be understood by consumers (e.g., Seldane does not produce drowsiness), and the potential effectiveness of DTC advertising (one survey indicated that 78% of consumers said they would be inclined to ask physicians about a drug they saw on TV; Scott-Levin survey cited in Davis, 1987).

Marketers also see problems with DTC advertising: it is difficult to design a sufficiently detailed balance statement (contra-indications) that does not inhibit sales; the FDA is inconsistent in its interpretation of what is required in a fairly balanced ad; consumer advertising is expensive; the possibility exists for patient lawsuits if a misdiagnosis occurs because the advertising is shown to be misleading or to interfere with the patient/physician relationship; and it is not clear how effective DTC ads will be (e.g., Scott-Levin found only 7% of consumers surveyed recalled seeing Pfizer "Partners in Healthcare" ads, and few were able to remember the theme of the ads).

COLLABORATION BETWEEN COMMERCIAL
AND PUBLIC HEALTH SECTORS

The collaboration of Kellogg's and the National Cancer Institute (NCI) is an effort to disseminate commercial health information through the mass media. As stated by a February 1987 editorial in the *American Journal of Public Health*, "A private company borrowed a health message from a government agency (with permission), devoted millions of dollars to its dissemination, and thereby increased its sales, while simultaneously conveying the agency's message to the public with a visibility the agency never could have achieved with its own resources."

Levy and Stokes (1987) conducted a study to determine the effects of Kellogg's use of specific health claims on the sales of high fiber cereals. Information was drawn from computerized purchase data from 209 Giant Food stores in metropolitan Baltimore and Washington, DC, over a 64-week period beginning 16 weeks prior to start of the campaign. Substantial increases were seen in purchases of Kellogg's high-fiber cereals. Sales of high-fiber cereals as a group increased, not just sales of Kellogg's high-fiber cereals. This was seen as indicating success in attracting new consumers to try high-fiber cereals in general, because of their fiber content, rather than simply redistributing existing demand in favor of Kellogg's brands.

A related issue is whether the campaign made new converts or simply attracted consumers already conscious of health issues away from old "all natural" products (e.g., granola cereals) to the newest generation of products being touted. To address this, NCI and FDA conducted two waves of telephone survey on cancer prevention and risk, before and after the Kellogg's campaign initiation; significantly more people reported eating more bran, fiber, and whole grains to reduce their cancer risk (Freimuth, Hammond, & Stein, 1988).

In 1986, a nationwide telephone survey conducted by the FDA and the National Heart, Lung, and Blood Institute (NHLBI) showed a 21% increase in the number of respondents who identified fiber as a preventive for cancer, compared to a 1984 survey conducted prior to the campaign; in addition, NCI reported substantial increases in inquiries from the general public to its Cancer Information Service tollfree line in the first year following the campaign (Freimuth, Hammond, & Stein, 1988).

The concept of linking commercial products with public sector endorsement is useful to both sides. Marketing corporations are eager to associate their brands with the authority and credibility of a government agency, a major nonprofit voluntary organization, or a professional medical association. Likewise, the public sector organizations are interested in the expanded communications reach, funding (and fundraising), and marketing skills that corporations can bring. Interestingly, from the public's point of view, the collaboration of a marketing corporation with a nonprofit source is perceived as almost as credible as a nonprofit source alone (Freimuth, Hammond, & Stein, 1988).

These alliances are growing more common, but require care in setting objectives, allocating the resources that each party will contribute, and protecting reputations.

SOCIAL RESPONSIBILITY IN MARKETING

Marketing companies and their advertising, public relations, and promotion departments and agencies are aware of social pressures and social responsibilities. These subjects are discussed constantly in the marketing literature and the trade media.

Companies are as familiar with pressures from social organizations (e.g., consumer activists, government legislators and regulators, religious and ethnic groups, media activists) as they are with pressures from their corporate competitors. A useful model was developed by Pearce (1979). It depicts the major groups involved in the public arena of marketing (government, advocates, competitors, and customers) and the nature of their interaction. Marketers are now being called on to be more socially responsible about the types of products they market and how these products are marketed. As stated by Pearce (1979, p. 10): "there has been a clear escalation in public expectations of marketing and business performance. . . . One of the key concepts is 'social responsibility,' which refers to performance beyond traditional economic performance. In addition to consumer interest, the public interest must be considered."

There are opportunities for health officials and corporations and their trade associations and agencies to work together to reach consensus—on particular issues—as to what public interest means and requires. What constitutes good and bad marketing performance in relation to quality of life? A company might market a "bad" product (e.g., cigarettes) in a "fair" manner (e.g., using only factual "tombstone advertising"). In another case, a "good" product (e.g., low-cholesterol margarine) might be promoted in a misleading way. Are potato chips, beer, wine coolers, candy, and presweetened cereals always "health compromising?" Few would argue that they are. But when do they present health concerns? And how should they be fairly presented in marketing communications?

Often, the public interest (what society "needs") conflicts with consumer interest (what the individual wants and buys). In such cases, industry codes and self-regulation, government intervention in the marketplace, and advocate pressures combine with profit squeezes, competitive activities, and cost-of-business factors to make judgments murky and difficult.

7

Regulatory Policies for Communicating Health Information

BRUCE A. SILVERGLADE

Both public and private regulatory policies often hinder the effective communication of public health information. These policies exist in many forms, ranging from official government regulations to informal programs operated by self-regulatory authorities. This chapter examines how such policies operate by focusing on attempts to communicate information in food advertising and labeling regarding the relationship between diet and disease.

PROMOTING HEALTH BENEFITS OF FOOD PRODUCTS

A consensus on the relationship between diet and disease has been building for the last two decades. The Surgeon General, in his recent report titled "Nutrition and Health," officially noted this consensus and advised the public to reduce its consumption of fat, cholesterol, and sodium and to increase its consumption of foods high in fiber, in order to reduce the risk of heart disease and cancer.

Not surprisingly, the food industry has identified a market advantage in promoting foods on the basis that they meet these guidelines for a healthy diet. Such promotion has primarily occurred in advertising and through the use of claims on food labels. Unfortunately, the food industry's attempts at bringing this information to consumers have resulted in a myriad of deceptive and misleading claims, thus diminishing the value of food advertising as an effective communications medium. According to a recent survey by the Consumer Network, only 16% of consumers now believe that food ads are "very honest," while 52% called them only "somewhat honest" or "dishonest." While the blame ultimately rests with unscrupulous marketers, a variety of public and private regulatory policies governing food advertising and labeling have certainly contributed to the problem. The evolution of policy-making has progressed through several stages over the past two decades.

ATTEMPTS AT "COMMAND AND CONTROL" REGULATORY TECHNIQUES

The federal agencies primarily concerned with regulating food advertising and labeling, the Federal Trade Commission (FTC), the Food and Drug Administration (FDA), and the U.S. Department of Agriculture (USDA), seriously began to analyze the regulatory implications of the growing scientific consensus on the relationship between diet and disease in the mid-1970s. The FDA, FTC, and USDA formed a tripartite task force to conduct a comprehensive investigation of how the food label could better communicate information that would help the consumer make more healthy food choices.

The Federal Trade Commission also proposed regulations governing how nutrition claims could be made in food advertising. The proposed rules attempted to control how nutritional comparisons between foods could be made. The rules also attempted to define minimum standards for foods claiming to be "nutritious," and to require disclosures of nutrition data in food advertising.

Most of these ambitious efforts failed. Each was based on traditional "command and control" regulatory techniques, and each ultimately fell victim to a food industry backlash against regulation.

ATTEMPTS TO CREATE A QUASI-GOVERNMENTAL INSTITUTION

In 1981, the FTC and the USDA joined with the food industry and consumer groups to create what came to be called the Network for Better Nutrition. The purpose of the network was to disseminate information to consumers regarding good nutritional practices and the relationship between diet and disease. The food industry consented to partially fund the network in order to head off the prospect of mandatory government regulation of food advertising. The network was formed at a very unfortunate time, however. After just a few months, it fell victim to the change in administrations. The USDA and the FTC withdrew, and the organization was disbanded in 1982.

RELIANCE ON FREE MARKET FORCES

After the Reagan administration assumed control of the FDA, FTC, and USDA, it became clear that reliance on free-market forces would be the primary strategy to ensure communication of health information to consumers. This strategy manifested itself in different ways at each of the agencies.

For example, the White House Office of Management and Budget pressured the FDA to rescind a regulation prohibiting disease prevention claims on food labels. This effort was initially triggered by a decision of the Kellogg's Company in 1984 to promote its *All-Bran* cereal as an important part of a high-fiber, low-fat diet, useful in reducing the risk of some forms of cancer. Administration officials were impressed with the educational potential of a large national advertising campaign and reasoned that the private sector could do a better job of informing the public about the relationship between diet and disease than could budget-strained federal agencies.

In 1987, after three years of dissension within the agency, the FDA formally proposed rescinding its traditional prohibition on disease prevention claims. The proposal was greeted with strong opposition from practically the entire medical and health communities.

The central problem with the FDA proposal was that it allowed food manufacturers to devise health claims of their own, without clearance from public health officials. Furthermore, the FDA proposal did not require that the claims be based on a consensus of scientific opinion, and it did not require the disclosure of nutritional drawbacks of the food product in question. The new health claim rule was supposed to harness the power of the food label and put it to work for the public health. It became clear, however, that the real effect of the rule, if implemented, would be to unleash a flurry of unsubstantiated claims on a vulnerable public.

Reliance on free-market forces has also made it difficult for the FDA to propose regulations defining low-fat or high-fiber foods. Consumers are increasingly seeking out such foods in order to comply with the advice of health specialists to reduce fat consumption and increase fiber intake.

Realizing that defining precise terms such as "low fat" and "high fiber" typically rests with the government, food manufacturers have coined a vague terminology to describe purportedly healthful foods. One popular term utilized by food marketers in advertising and labeling is "light." Surveys taken by the Food and Drug Administration reveal that most consumers believe that so-called light foods are lower in fat, sodium, or calories than regular foods. Unfortunately, many food companies misleadingly label products as "light" even though they are no healthier than traditional products. The companies, when asked, say that the products are lighter in color, taste, or texture, or even that the suggested serving size is simply smaller!

DECLINE IN "SELF-REGULATION"

The laissez-faire policy of administration officials has had a direct effect on self-regulatory authorities. The National Advertising Division (NAD) of the Council of the Better Business Bureaus reviews complaints concerning advertising from both competitors and consumers. The NAD was formed in the early 1970s, when the Federal Trade Commission was known for aggressive regulation.

During this era of federal deregulation, the NAD has begun to show signs of institutional decay. In the late 1980s, the agency handled about 90 cases per year, approximately one-third less than it managed at the beginning of the decade. The decrease in caseload has occurred notwithstanding an increase in expenditures on advertising, as well as an increase in the incidence of misleading claims.

A related development has occurred with the broadcast standards and clearance offices of the three major television networks, which review ads to ensure that they are not deceptive. Two of the three networks were taken over by larger companies that control businesses outside the communications industry. These new owners installed a bottom-line corporate mentality that is insensitive to public interest considerations that had been taken relatively seriously by network managers. The new corporate officers argued that the networks need not spend large sums operating their own self-regulatory bureaus since the federal government itself was no longer placing a premium on regulating deceptive advertising. Accordingly, the staffs of these network offices were cut by one-half or more. With such skeleton staffs, it has been practically impossible to review the thousands of different commercials aired on network television each year and the hundreds of formal challenges submitted by aggrieved competitors and consumers.

UNILATERAL EFFORTS BY PUBLIC HEALTH AGENCIES AND PRIVATE ORGANIZATIONS

Understandably, the public health community has responded to these failures by trying to bypass both the federal and self-regulatory processes. The National Cancer Institute (NCI), for example, began working directly with food marketers to educate the public about the relationship between fiber and cancer (see Novelli, Chapter 6). The NCI was instrumental in facilitating the well-known ad campaign by Kellogg's that promoted its *All-Bran* cereal as an important part of a high-fiber, low-fat diet, useful in reducing the risk of certain forms of cancer. The NCI/Kellogg's initiative "end-runned" the Food and Drug Administration which, up until that time, completely prohibited disease prevention claims on food labels.

Overall, the NCI/Kellogg's initiative was educational and informative, yet the project opened a Pandora's box of misleading claims by other food companies trying to mimic Kellogg's success. For example, in 1987 the Campbell Soup company approached the NCI about making the same high-fiber, low-fat diet/cancer claim for its bean and pea soups. After informing the NCI of its intent, Campbell developed a similar advertising campaign, which expressly referenced the NCI dietary recommendations. Not only did the NCI not consent to this advertisement, the agency strenuously objected when the ads began to appear. In late 1987, the NCI wrote the Campbell Soup company and explained that it felt the ads were misleading since the product was high in sodium, and thus, in the NCI's view, not a healthy source of fiber. Furthermore, the NCI noted that several varieties of the bean and pea soups contained meats such as bacon, which the NCI felt could deliver an overall confusing message to consumers trying to reduce the risk of cancer by making dietary modifications.

Campbell Soup demurred from the NCI's complaints and claimed the ads were not misleading. Ultimately, all the NCI could do was to insist that its name be taken out of the advertisements and to refer the matter to a less than enthusiastic FTC. In 1988, the FTC brought suit against Campbell Soup on another claim in the same ad, which concerned the relationship of a low-fat/low-cholesterol diet to heart disease, but the FTC never challenged the low fat/high fiber cancer claim.

The danger in such promotions by public health agencies is that these agencies have no legal authority to control abuses. The Campbell Soup debacle is a prime example.

Other nongovernmental organizations have faced other problems dealing with private industry. In 1987, the Fleischmann's Margarine division of RJR Nabisco asked the American Academy of Family Physicians to join in a $1 million anti-heart disease campaign. The academy insisted that the campaign warn consumers that smoking, as well as poor diet, promotes heart disease. When the press independently exposed the project, pointing out that it would be the first time that a tobacco company voluntarily admitted that cigarettes cause heart disease, Fleischmann's pulled out of the deal.

Similarly, in 1986, the American Heart Association approached *Reader's Digest* to run an ad supplement highlighting the dangers of tobacco. *Reader's Digest* is one of the few national magazines that accepts no tobacco advertising, but it does accept food advertising. The *Chicago Sun-Times* reported that pressure from General Foods, which is owned by Philip Morris, killed the proposal.

The American Heart Association also has announced a program whereby it will license the use of its heart symbol on foods deemed by the association to fit in a heart-healthy diet. The AHA plan has been criticized by the federal government and some segments of the food industry. Similar certification programs operated in the past by the American Medical Association, and others, have not been successful.

OPTIONS FOR THE FUTURE

While this litany of failed or troubled initiatives may pose a seemingly insurmountable obstacle to effective communication of health information in food advertising and labeling, additional alternatives do exist. The most obvious is a federal appropriation of say $150 million that would be used to pay for a sustained media campaign, educating the public about the relationship between diet and disease.

In light of the chronic federal budget deficit, such expensive campaigns may be unrealistic. Thus, it is necessary to consider programs not relying solely on an increase in federal expenditures, such as a new public-private partnership. Several points should be kept in mind, however.

First, history tells us that such partnerships work only if they operate under the threat of mandatory government regulation. If such a threat is politically unrealistic, federal agencies may wish to trade a few "carrots" in other areas of concern to the food industry, such as speedy regulatory approvals, for greater industry cooperation in an educational campaign. It is important that a federal agency with legal authority to regulate the industry participants must be involved in the process. This is essential in case the industry members are tempted, as a result of the normal pressures of the marketplace, to promote their own interests over the public interest. The operations of the partnership should be open to the public, and participation should be balanced among all interested parties.

Another option for the future may involve state governments. In recent years, state attorneys general have been active in stopping deceptive health and nutrition claims in food advertising and labeling. The state agencies involved with these initiatives may be willing to contribute settlement funds to public education efforts. The expenditure of these funds for this purpose would help educate the public about the relationship between diet and disease, as well as to correct some of the misleading impressions left by deceptive ads and labels.

CONCLUSION

Regulatory policies ranging from traditional attempts at "command and control" to laissez-faire free-market approaches have hindered the effective communication of health information in food advertising and labeling. As a result, public and private health organizations have increased their own attempts to harness the power of food ads and labels to educate the public. Such attempts are risky, given the reality that such groups lack the authority to enforce their programs.

Future efforts to educate the public would ideally be made a national priority and receive appropriate levels of funding from the federal government. If a federal commitment of this magnitude cannot be obtained, a new public-private partnership between the government and the food industry might be attempted. This latter effort might work if a credible threat of mandatory regulation is present, or it could be facilitated by federal agencies trading inducements in other areas of regulatory concern to the food industry for cooperation in nutrition education programs.

8

Television and Health:
Images and Impact

NANCY SIGNORIELLI

Television is our most common and constant learning environment. Its world both mirrors and leads society. Television is first and foremost a storyteller—it tells most of the stories to most of the people most of the time—and thus it is the wholesale distributor of images, and it forms the mainstream of our popular culture. Our children are born into a home in which a centralized commercial institution, rather than parents, church, or school, tells most of the stories. The world of television shows and tells us about life—people, places, striving, power, and fate. This storytelling function of television is extremely important, for it is through these stories that people learn many different things about the world and its peoples.

TV's entertainment programs and commercials, with potential health messages embedded in them, reach tens of millions of viewers each day. More importantly, these messages reach viewers who would otherwise not expose themselves to such information and do not fully realize that these messages may impact upon them.

Recent public health evidence demonstrates the importance of life-style factors, including the media's influence in both imparting health information and impacting upon health. According to the Surgeon General, culturally sustained behavioral and life-style factors account for as much as half of U.S. mortality (*Healthy People*, 1979).

The success or failure of education programs and information campaigns depend largely on the broader cultural context into which they are injected. Few campaigns can succeed without knowing what they are up against. Today, that means knowing what messages and images television and other mass media discharge into the mainstream of common consciousness.

This review will focus upon these messages—what is known about health portrayals and their potential lessons for viewers. The review primarily focuses on television and examines a number of specific substantive areas. It is organized by topic, looking first at the images to which people are exposed and then at the research (where available) that has examined the impact of these images on people's conceptions relating to health matters.

ILLNESS ON TELEVISION

What kind of health-related information do we get when we watch television? Smith, Trivax, Zuehlke, Lowinger, and Nghiem (1972) examined 130 hours of programming broadcast during one week in 1970, evaluating all items (entertainment, news, commercials, etc.) relating to mental or physical illness, doctors, dentists, medical treatment, smoking, or health. Overall, this analysis revealed that health-related content appeared in 7% of the programming, but less than one-third was useful information. In fact, 70% of the health material was inaccurate, misleading, or both. Messages urging the use of pills or other drug-related remedies outnumbered messages against drug use or abuse by 10:1. In this week of programming, major health problems such as cancer, heart disease, stroke, accidents, hepatitis, venereal disease, mental health, and sex education were practically ignored.

Heeter, Perlstadt, and Greenberg (1984), in an analysis of the 10 top-rated prime-time fictional series broadcast in the 1979-1980 season, found that medical and health-related content appeared with considerable frequency, with an average of 5.5 health-related scenes per hour. These episodes typically involved current health problems of older adults, young children, and women, and were mentioned rather than featured in the story line. The depictions were not very informative, treatment and overall concern of the physician was not heroic, and patients were rarely shown interacting with their doctor. Heeter et al. also noted that the cost of medical care was never mentioned: characters looked for and received the best medical care with no apparent financial consequence.

Over the 17 years that the Cultural Indicators project (Gerbner, Morgan, & Signorielli, 1982; Signorielli, 1985, 1987) has been monitoring trends in network dramatic programming, 40% of programs and 8% of the major characters in prime-time programs have been presented as physically ill (having illnesses or injuries that have required medical treatment). Physical illness is rarer in children's weekend daytime programming, as only 3% of these major characters get injured or sick enough to require some type of medical treatment. Illness and injury seem to affect heroes and villains, males and females, young and old, and other groups of characters quite similarly.

Turow and Coe (1985), in an examination of 14 days of network programming (morning news, soap operas, evening news, prime time, and commercials), found that television medicine had little in common with recent changes in U.S. health care (e.g., the importance of chronic illnesses, rising costs, hospitals' desire for frugality, competition for patients whose ability to pay is unaffected by declining federal and state payment policy). This analysis revealed that one third of illness-related coverage was found in commercials for pharmaceutical products, especially cold and pain remedies. Prime-time network programming accounted for another 3rd of coverage, daytime serials made up almost a 5th, news magazines more than a 10th, and evening news broadcasts less than one-20th. No matter in which program illness appeared, however, it took center stage: almost 9 out of 10 interactions involving ill people revolved around their maladies.

Turow and Coe also found that almost none of the television portrayals presented the illness as chronic. Television focused upon acute illness that can be cured (even if the doctor has to go to heroic ends). Moreover, attempts to deal with the illness focused upon biomedical-, pharmacological-, or technological-related cures rather than interpersonal or psychological factors. In addition, the hospital was the location for the professional treatment of illness; medical personnel aside from physicians and nurses were ignored; and medical care "was portrayed as overwhelmingly appropriate, nonpolitical, and an unlimited resource" (Turow & Coe, 1985, p. 47)—a far cry from the reality of health care in the United States.

Images of Cancer and AIDS

News coverage of cancer is an important source of information for many people. A survey sponsored by the American Cancer Society found that 82% of respondents cited television, 65% newspapers, 61% magazines, and 42% radio as cancer information sources (see Freimuth, Greenberg, DeWitt, & Romano, 1984).

An examination of news coverage about cancer (Freimuth et al., 1984) revealed that the headlines of news stories about cancer are generally accurate and neutral in tone, but that the stories themselves do not provide statistics about the incidence of cancer. Stories tend to focus upon cancer in general rather than cancer of a specific part of the body. News coverage also tends to emphasize dying rather than coping, and little information is given about resources (psychological, financial, or organizational). In addition, the stories do not provide information about prevention, risks, detection, and the treatment of cancer (prevention was discussed in only 5% of the stories). Similarly, newspaper health columns usually mention cancer of a nonspecific origin. Most columns focus upon causes or the detection of cancer, while few mention treatments of physical consequences of the disease.

Dearing and Rogers (1988) examined what the public said that they knew about Acquired Immune Deficiency Syndrome. Archival data showed that public awareness about AIDS diffused rapidly and early, but that a certain degree of confusion existed among the U.S. public about modes of AIDS transmission, reflecting ambiguity and even reversals in scientific research results and statements. Relative to other health problems in the United States, AIDS is considered by far the most important, and more government spending on AIDS is favored by a majority of the U.S. public.

TELEVISION DOCTORS AND NURSES

Even though characters are seldom physically ill on television, the world of television has a large number of doctors and nurses. In fact, a special analysis of the Cultural Indicators data bank revealed that between 1973 and 1985, among the major characters there were 103 doctors, 13 psychiatrists, and 28 nurses, for 228 physically ill and 88 mentally ill characters. This is a ratio of one doctor for almost every two patients.

Health professionals (doctors and nurses) dominate the ranks of TV professionals, numbering almost five times their real-life proportions. Only criminals or law enforcers are more numerous in the world of television. Visible as health professionals are in network prime-time programming, they are virtually absent from network weekend-daytime (children's) programs.

Doctors probably fare best of all occupations on television. Compared to other professionals, they are relatively good, successful, and peaceful. Less than 4% of television doctors (major characters) are evil, which is half the number found in other professions. Personality ratings show doctors a bit more fair, sociable, and warm than most other characters. Doctors are also rated smarter and more rational, stable, and fair than are nurses.

McLaughlin (1975) found that doctors symbolize authority, power, and knowledge; they dominate and control the lives of others. In addition, doctors are easily accessible to patients, command nurses (who never disobey their orders), advise each other, but rarely receive advice from patients or orders from superiors (and, when they do, they often disregard them). Yet they are also honest, courageous, kind, ethical, and responsive to the requests of their patients. Television doctors often risk status or prestige to perform an unusual or dangerous treatment; they also disobey rules and conventions, always succeeding against odds to treat or cure some disease or settle some crisis.

FOOD AND NUTRITION

The quantity and quality of food commercials on children's television were well-documented in research conducted through the 1970s. During a typical year, the average child viewer will see about 22,000 commercials, 5,000 of them for food products, over half which are high-calorie, high-sugar, low-nutrition items (Choate, 1975, 1976).

Commercials geared for the child audience stress fun and tend to be fast-paced with enchanting music, jingles, fantasy, humor, and appealing characters (Barcus, 1980; Goldberg & Gorn, 1978). In addition, most of the ads do not mention sweetness or make nutritional claims, while one-fourth mention premiums associated with the product (Atkin & Heald, 1977).

In prime-time programming, nutrition is anything but balanced or relaxed. Grabbing a snack (39% of all eating-drinking episodes) is virtually as frequent as breakfast, lunch, and dinner combined (42%). Kaufman (1980) analyzed messages relating to food, eating behavior, and ideal body images in the 10 top-rated prime-time programs and found that there are more food representations in programs than commercials. A point-by-point comparison of eating behavior on television along nutritional guidelines exposed the contradictions between the dramatic requirements and motivations (such as reward, punishment, bribe) and recommended eating habits. Kaufman also found that television characters are usually happy when around food, rarely dine alone, and often snack. Food is never explicitly used to satisfy hunger; rather it is used for social and emotional purposes.

An analysis of prime-time and weekend-daytime commercials (Gerbner, Gross, Morgan, & Signorielli, 1981) revealed that food advertising accounts for more than one quarter of such commercials. Sweets, snacks, and nonnutritious ("junk") foods make up nearly half of food commercials. Nutritional appeals are noted in only 9% and stressed in another 7% of food commercials.

Overall, the message about nutrition presented on television is not healthy. Production techniques contribute to a happy, positive, and fun attitude toward advertised foods. Programming rarely incorporates meals, and snacks are consumed more for social and emotional purposes than to satisfy hunger. Finally, dietary recommendations (eat a variety of foods; maintain desirable weight; avoid too much fat, saturated fat, and cholesterol; eat foods with adequate starch and fiber; avoid too much sugar and sodium; based on Peterkin, 1985) often are the opposite of the foods that make up a major portion of the "diet" in the television world.

Heavy viewing has been shown to be related to low nutritional knowledge and incorrect perceptions about the validity of nutrition claims in food commercials, as well as greater consumption of nonnutritious foods, such as candy, salty snacks, and desserts (Atkin, 1976, 1980; Clancy-Hepburn, Hickey, & Neville, 1974).

Examining the impact of Saturday morning commercials, Atkin and Gibson (1978) found that frequent exposure to ads contributed little to children's understanding of the "balanced breakfast" concept. Donohue (1975) found that black children believed that to maintain good health they should take advertised medicines, eat vitamins, drink Coke, and eat fast foods. In addition, Donohue, Meyer, and Henke (1978) found that 7 out of 10 children thought that fast foods (e.g., McDonald's) were more nutritious than the food they had at home.

Goldberg, Gorn, and Gibson (1978) found that children who saw commercials for sugared snacks and cereals were more likely to choose sugared foods, while children who viewed PSAs focusing on nutrition chose more nutritious foods. Moreover, this study revealed that when exposure to sugar-related commercials was doubled, there was a corresponding increase in the preferred number of nonadvertised foods containing sugar. Roberts and his colleagues (Roberts & Bachen, 1978; Roberts, Gibson & Bachen, 1979) found that children who saw PSAs about nutrition had higher scores on a test of nutrition knowledge than the children who did not see these PSAs. Finally, Bolton's (1983) study of households with children aged 2 to 11 found that the children's exposure to television food advertising slightly influenced their diets by increasing the number of snacks and decreasing nutrient efficiency.

Goldberg, Gorn, and Gibson (1978) found that both PSAs and programs that promote good health practices and nutrition influenced both intended and actual food choices of children. Children who saw an episode of *Fat Albert* about problems related to eating junk food chose significantly fewer sugared foods than the children who did not see this program. This research also revealed that children who saw PSAs for healthy foods were more likely to choose these types of foods than the children who were exposed to commercials for foods high in sugar content. Finally, research has shown that children are able to recall and make sense of disclosures about the problems associated with eating too much candy and sugared cereals (Faber, Meyer, & Miller, 1984).

Even though there are so many portrayals of unhealthy and fattening foods, obesity (a problem that plagues at least 25% of the American population) claims few victims on television. The dramatic functions of being fat are limited to certain characterizations, often further aggravating its prejudicial associations. Consequently almost all of the characters on television are slim, sporting the ideal body weight and proportion. According to Gerbner, Gross, Morgan, and Signorielli (1981), less than 6% of all males and 2% of all females on television were obese.

On a more general level, there are also indications that exposure to television's portrayal of health images may contribute to health-related knowledge and behaviors. Gerbner, Morgan, and Signorielli (1982) present evidence that unhealthy practices may accompany greater reliance upon television for health information. In an analysis of data collected in a study conducted by General Mills, respondents were given a list of 16 information sources (doctors, friends, families, television programs, popular books on health, etc.) and asked which were their "two or three main sources" of health information. "Television programs" were the second-most cited sources (chosen by 31%), led only by "doctors and dentists" (chosen by 45%).

More important, those who did choose television programs manifested a distinct profile. They were significantly more likely to be "complacent" on health attitudes, hold "old" health values, be "nonexercisers" on physical fitness, and "poorly informed" about health. Gerbner et al. (1982) also analyzed data collected in a Roper study and found that those who watched more television were more likely to say that they were not concerned about weight; they ate and drank whatever they wanted, whenever they wanted.

Although these findings do not prove that television contributes to poor health routines and lack of awareness of health information, they do suggest that persons who credit television as a main source of information are not among the more health-minded segments of the population.

There is some evidence indicating a relationship between television viewing and obesity. Dietz and Gortmaker (1985) and Dietz (1989), in an analysis of data for samples of children and adolescents in two National Health Examination Surveys, found a significant association between time spent watching television and the prevalence of obesity and superobesity. Tucker (1986), however, did not find a significant relationship between television viewing and obesity, but did find a significant relationship between television viewing and lower measures of physical fitness.

IMPAIRMENT AND SAFETY

Characters in prime-time programming are not only healthy, they are also relatively safe from accidents and rarely suffer impairment of any function (few even wear glasses). Despite all the violence on television, in prime-time programs industrial accidents and highway crashes—the leading causes of violent injury and death in America—are rare. Moreover television characters rarely take precautions against them.

Greenberg and Atkin's (1983) analysis of four week-long samples of prime-time programming revealed that driving took place at the rate of 4.5 incidents per hour of programming, with half of the programs (usually action-adventure genre) having driving scenes. While many of these scenes involved routine business, there was a substantial number of chase and escape scenes involving sedans and police cars, and few drivers fastened or wore a seat belt. While driving acts that endangered people appeared 0.7 times per hour, death and injury were relatively rare.

SMOKING

The impression of some that television characters smoke a great deal is unwarranted and may be a result of recollections of the older shows and movies produced during the years that smoking was much more commonplace. Breed and De Foe (1984) found that between 1950 and 1982 there was a steady drop in the use of cigarettes in entertainment television programming. In the years before the Surgeon General's 1964 report on smoking, characters smoked nine times more cigarettes than they smoked in programs broadcast during the 1982 television season.

Other analyses support the low incidence of smoking on television. Greenberg, Fernandez-Collado, Korzenny, and Atkin (1979) observed that an average TV viewer must watch two hours to see someone smoke a cigar, cigarette, or pipe. Gerbner, Morgan, and Signorielli's (1982) special analysis of data from the Cultural Indicators data archives revealed that, among major characters in prime-time programs, only 11% of the men and 2% of the women smoked. In addition, Signorielli's (1987) analysis of this data base showed that major characters who drank were also likely to smoke, and that 13 of the 34 alcoholics were smokers.

These few studies also indicate that television programs rarely show characters refusing to smoke or expressing antismoking sentiments. More than likely, as has been documented in regard to print media (Smith, 1978; Weis & Burke, 1986; Warner, 1985), there is also an unwritten agreement to refrain from anti-smoking messages so as not to offend the cigarette companies who spend many millions of dollars on commercials for their noncigarette products such as beer and foods.

Since the ban on advertising cigarette and other tobacco products in broadcast media was instituted in 1971, the print media have enjoyed huge increases in revenue from cigarette advertisements. In fact, in comparison with other consumer products, cigarettes are the most widely advertised; in 1983, $1.5 billion was devoted to their promotion (Warner, 1985). Because of this, the editorial policy of many magazines is to play down the hazards of smoking by not publishing articles focusing upon the dangers of smoking.

For example, a study of 10 prominent women's magazines (that also depend upon cigarette advertisements for revenue) found that between 1967 and 1979 only 8 feature articles discussed the dangers of smoking and 4 of the 10 magazines carried no antismoking articles at all. In comparison, *Good Housekeeping* and *Seventeen*, two magazines that do not accept cigarette advertising, published 11 and 5 articles respectively (Whelan, Sheridan, Meister, & Mosher, 1981). In addition, *Reader's Digest*, which also does not accept cigarette advertising, has a good track record in providing thorough coverage of the health hazards of smoking.

There have also been reports that two of the most widely read and influential news magazines, *Time* and *Newsweek*, have actually deleted text adverse to smoking from special supplements about personal health care (Warner, 1985; Weis & Burke, 1986). Moreover, Smith (1978) reports that between 1971 and 1978 neither *Time* nor *Newsweek* published a comprehensive report about the health hazards of smoking although they reported, in bits and pieces, new evidence linking disease to smoking.

One area of research has examined the processes by which these advertisers try to persuade young people and women to smoke (Altman, Slater, Albright, & Maccoby, 1987). This study revealed that advertisements in women's magazines tend to emphasize erotic images, while those in magazines for young people focus upon images of recreation, adventure, and risk. Thus, these ads seem to imply an association of cigarette smoking with health, vitality, and sexiness; consequently, an implicit goal may be to allay consumer concerns about safety of smoking.

ALCOHOL

Over the past two decades, Signorielli (1987) found a steady increase in the number of references to alcohol (talking about, showing characters drinking). The percentage of programs making some reference to alcohol ranged from a low of 10% in 1969 to over 70% in the more recent samples. While the percentage of programs mentioning the harmful effects of alcohol increased from less than 5% to 25% of the yearly sample, the number of alcoholics remained about the same (1% to 2% of the major characters in each yearly sample). Similarly,

Wallack, Breed and Cruz (1987) found that 80% of prime-time programs in a sample of 1984 programming contained one or more appearances of alcohol and that alcohol was actually ingested on 60% of the
programs. In this sample, most drinking took place in dramas at the rate
of 11 specific acts of drinking per hour. Wallack et al. concluded that a
regular viewer of dramas would be likely to see more than 20 specific
acts of drinking during an evening's viewing.

Drinking is also a regular and frequent occurrence in the daytime
serial dramas; drinking levels, however, are substantially below those
isolated in analyses of prime-time programming (Greenberg, 1981;
Wallack, Breed, & De Foe, 1985). MacDonald (1983) found that, in
soap operas, alcohol was the most frequently mentioned "drug" and
that, contrary to statistics on the U.S. population, more women than men
were portrayed as alcoholics or problem drinkers and that most of the
alcoholics belonged to the upper-middle class rather than working class.

Drinking on television is usually not a casual affair of one or two
drinks. Breed and De Foe (1981) analyzed 233 scenes about alcohol in
prime-time drama and found that 40% consisted of five or more drinks
and 18% involved chronic drinkers. More recent evidence shows de-
clines in heavy drinking (Wallack, Grube, Madden, & Breed, in press).

Alcoholic beverages not only outnumber other beverages consumed
on television but the pattern of drinking is virtually the inverse of the
pattern in daily life. Alcohol drinking acts were more than twice as
frequent as the second-ranking coffee and tea, 14 times as frequent as
soft drinks, and more than 15 times as frequent as water. Of all identifiable alcoholic beverages, 52% were hard liquor, 22% were wine, and
16% were beer.

Signorielli's (1987) analysis revealed that more than one-third of the
major characters in prime-time programming are social drinkers. Men
and women are equally likely to drink. Those who drink are more likely
than those who do not drink to be involved in a romantic relationship.
Alcoholics, on the other hand, while small in number, differ consider-
ably from the typical character social drinker on television. Alcoholics
are more likely to be men, are much more likely to be involved in
violence, and tend to have negative personality traits.

Breed and De Foe (1981) found that characters seldom refused a
drink or indicated any type of disapproval of drinking. If and when
disapproval was expressed, it was mild, ineffective, came from women,
and was directed at women and teenage drinkers. Breed and De Foe
also found that while drinking was seldom rationalized or excused in

dramas, it often was in situation comedies. Moreover, in this genre, intoxication and hangovers were usually treated humorously. The most frequent reason for drinking on television is a personal crisis. For the most part, the harmful effects or consequences of drinking are rarely presented adequately (Signorielli, 1987).

Daytime serials, however, present a more realistic picture of alcohol as a potentially harmful and problematic substance (Greenberg, 1981; Wallack, Breed, & De Foe, 1985). Specifically, Wallack et al. (1985) found that one serial drama, *All My Children*, accurately portrayed drinking problems, presented a number of good role models for social drinking and abstinence, and frequently presented negative reinforcement (and even positive interventions by other characters) for characters who took part in heavy or high-risk drinking.

Analyses of commercials for alcoholic beverages reveal that commercials for beer predominate. Atkin, Hocking, and Block et al. (1984) summarize research indicating that many of the commercials for alcoholic beverages imply that alcohol can be consumed in great quantities, few commercials suggest moderation in drinking, and none mentions any harmful effects. In addition, a nationwide survey of 1,200 respondents between 12 and 22 years of age revealed that alcohol advertising appears to contribute to certain forms of problem drinking; there is a moderate positive correlation between exposure to advertisements for wine, beer, and liquor and excessive consumption of alcoholic beverages as well as drinking in a hazardous situation, such as automobile driving (Atkin, Neuendorf, & McDermott, 1983).

In a similar study, teenagers were asked about their exposure to TV and magazine advertising for beer, wine, and liquor (Atkin, Hocking, & Block, 1984). The results revealed significant relationships between exposure and drinking behavior, especially for liquor and beer. These authors also found that peer influence seemed to play a larger role in wine and beer drinking while advertising had a greater contribution in regard to liquor drinking.

DRUGS

While images relating to drinking and alcohol abound on television and in other media, images relating to drugs and drug abuse are relatively rare. Research by numerous investigators (e.g., De Foe, Breed, & Wallack, 1983; Greenberg et al., 1979, 1980; Gerbner et al., 1981) indicates that illicit drug use and abuse seldom occur in entertainment programming; depictions typically focus on the illegal nature of drugs, and the action often revolves around "catching" the drug pushers. Finally, work conducted as part of the Cultural Indicators project analyzing annual weeklong samples of prime-time and weekend-daytime programming broadcast between 1969 and 1985 revealed few mentions of drugs use; about 3% of the major characters were portrayed as drug addicts.

OVER-THE-COUNTER MEDICINES

While images relating to illegal drugs are rare, there are numerous references to over-the-counter medicines. These references seldom appear in entertainment programming; rather, most depictions are found in commercials. According to Hanneman and McEwen (1976), these commercials for over-the-counter medicines greatly outnumbered any sort of PSAs about drug abuse. Moreover, such messages generally were aired at the optimal viewing times.

McEwen and Hanneman (1974) also found that few commercial messages warn of the possible dangers from the abuse of prescription or over-the-counter medicines. In addition, these messages usually emphasize, specifically or through the sequences of changes in the demeanor of the character, some promised psychological or social benefit beyond simple physical benefits from taking the drug.

Barcus (1976) found that commercials for drug products were advertised at a rate of one per hour. Internal analgesics, such as aspirin, were the most prominent (25%), followed by antihistamine preparations, antacids, laxatives, vitamin and mineral preparations, sleeping aids, etc. The analysis revealed that 80% to 90% of the commercials made a reference to specific ailments, conditions, or symptoms for which the drug was intended. The ads offered not only specific relief but also relaxation, general well-being ("look better," "feel younger"), or the maintenance of one's overall health. Psychological well-being and mood changes (frowns turned to smiles) were also indicated.

One of the major concerns is whether these entertainment and advertising images have an impact on legal and illicit drug use and/or abuse. Milavsky, Pekowsky, and Stipp (1975-1976), in a modified panel study of both illicit drug and proprietary medicine use among teenage boys, found a positive but relatively weak relationship between exposure to proprietary advertising and reported medicine use. In addition, this relationship was accentuated in homes in which there were numerous proprietary medicines available and where the mother initiates dispensing of medicines. These authors also found a negative relationship between exposure to drug advertising on television and the use of illicit drugs.

Atkin (1978), using a convenience sample of youngsters between 10 and 12, found that as exposure to advertising for medicines increases, children perceive that people are sick more often, worry about getting sick, approve of medicine, and are more likely to report that they feel better after taking medicine. Atkin found no relationship between exposure to medicine advertising and usage patterns. Finally, interviews with mother-child dyads (Robertson, Rossiter, & Gleason, 1979; Rossiter & Robertson, 1980) yielded limited evidence of a relationship between exposure to medicine commercials and the child's belief in the efficacy of medicine, the intent to take medicine when ill, and requesting medicine from a parent.

SEX AND SEXUALITY

Sexual socialization is a topic of considerable concern in our society. Traditionally, the common assumption is that information about sex and sexuality should be transmitted within the family, thus allowing for a maintenance of moral values and understanding. In reality, however, many parents are reticent or embarrassed to talk to their children about "the facts of life." Thus, adolescents are caught in the dilemma of wanting to know about sex—what is happening to their bodies, how to have a relationship with someone, how to know when they are "in love," and just what sexual activity entails—and often rely upon their peers, who are often equally misinformed, for information about sex (Strouse & Fabes, 1985).

The media, because of their nonthreatening, storytelling style, are an important source of sexual material for children and adolescents. Until recently, the media have also been reticent or perhaps unable to mention teenage pregnancy and/or sexually transmitted disease and to offer information that might help combat these problems.

Signorielli (1987) found that since the late 1970s the amount of sex on prime-time dramatic programs has remained at consistently high levels, occurring in 9 out of 10 programs. This analysis of eight annual weeklong samples of prime-time network dramatic programming revealed that sex was incidental to the plot in 60% of these programs and a major or significant plot feature in 35% of the programs. One quarter of all sexual references on television were light or comic in nature; sexual references were especially prevalent in situation comedies.

The daytime serial dramas have traditionally relied upon sex and sexual liaisons, intricacies, and disillusionments as part of their continuing stories. Greenberg, Abelman, and Neuendorf (1981) found that sexual relations were most likely to occur between partners who were not married to each other, and that sexual acts and references occurred quite frequently. Greenberg et al. (1986a; 1986b; 1987) also found that in those serial dramas most popular with adolescents, the rates of sexual content have grown steadily since 1980; in 1985 the average adolescent viewer was exposed to about 2,000 sexual references.

Music videos have emerged as a medium designed almost exclusively for adolescents and young adults. Sherman and Dominick (1986) found that sexual intimacy, much of it adolescent and titillating, appeared in three-quarters of the videos at a rate of almost five acts per video. Sex in the videos was seldom overt and usually traditional: most of the sexual acts were flirtations and nonintimate touching.

Contraception and sexually transmitted diseases are topics that have been ignored in entertainment media. Lowry and Towles (1989), in an analysis of daytime serial dramas, found that there were no instances (verbal, physical, or implied) of pregnancy contraception or the prevention of sexually transmitted diseases. While the overall message of the soap operas is that sex is for unmarried partners, the programs imply that it is not necessary to be concerned about preventing pregnancy or sexually transmitted diseases.

A number of laboratory studies have revealed relationships between viewing sexually explicit materials and accepting less stringent views about sex. Greeson and Williams (1986) found that after seeing less than an hour of videos on MTV, adolescents in the 7th and 12th grades were more likely to approve of premarital sex than their peers who had not seen the music videos. In addition, Zillmann and Bryant (in press), in studies of male and female college students, found that exposure to nonviolent sexually explicit films was related to the acceptance of promiscuity and sexual infidelity.

There have been few studies focusing upon the relationship between television viewing and initiation of sexual intercourse. Peterson, Moore, and Furstenberg (in press) found that, among a panel of adolescent boys, there was a relationship between viewing programs high in sexual content, measured during a first wave of data collection, and the subsequent initiation of sexual activity. A similar relationship was not isolated for the girls. Brown and Newcomer (in press) found that those adolescents who watched television programs that were "sexy" were more likely to have had sexual intercourse in the preceding year. Brown, Childers, and Waszak (1989) note that this study could not answer the question of whether viewing led to sexual behavior or whether being sexually active lead to the viewing of more sexually explicit materials.

CONCLUSIONS AND SUGGESTIONS FOR FURTHER RESEARCH

There is a considerable amount of health-related information in television programming and commercials. Much of the research reveals that these images are often in serious conflict with realistic guidelines for health and medicine. Research on the contributions of these portrayals to people's conceptions about health and medicine, however, is scarce.

On television, when illness occurs, it takes center stage and tends to be presented as acute, and (except in some daytime serial dramas) a cure is readily achieved with no consideration of the costs involved. Medical care, in the form of all-powerful physicians, abounds, while support staff, mainly deferential nurses and paramedics, lags behind. Overall, as Turow and Coe (1985) indicate, television medicine has little in common with recent changes in U.S. health care.

Television also provides unhealthy messages about food, nutrition, and weight. Food, whether in a commercial or in a story, is presented in a fun-oriented context: it satisfies emotional or social purposes rather than hunger. Grabbing a snack, usually a sweet, is as prevalent as sitting down to a meal. Overall, the "diet" of the television world is quite the opposite of current dietary recommendations. Finally, despite the starch and sweet-filled television diet, hardly anyone on television is even slightly overweight. Research reveals that children are affected by nutrition-related messages (whether pro- or anti-nutrition). Those who watch more television, or are more likely to cite television as a source of health-related information, tend to have poor nutritional knowledge and behavior patterns.

Characters in prime-time programming are not only healthy (though often vulnerable to violence-related injuries) but also relatively safe from accidents, hardly ever need glasses (even in old age), and rarely suffer impairment of any function.

Smoking and illegal drug use on television are also relatively rare. Illegal drug use is usually presented in the context of law enforcement, with the pusher or user apprehended in the climax of the story. Drinking, however, is hard to miss (characters are as likely to have an alcoholic drink as coffee, tea, milk, or a soft drink), and its appearance has steadily increased over the last 30 years. For the most part, the harmful effects or consequences of drinking too much are not presented adequately. However, we know little about the impact of dramatic messages relating to drinking, smoking, and drug use upon people's conceptions about these things.

Finally, while sex abounds on television, messages relating to sexually transmitted diseases and condom use are rarely presented. In addition, most of the sexual images are adolescent in nature, focusing upon titillation and stressing the comic nature of sexuality.

The research reveals that, for the most part, we have adequate baseline information about how health-related issues are presented on television. Nevertheless, there are numerous areas that have not been examined in sufficient detail. For example, in relation to smoking and drinking, we need to know the degree to which these things are incidental to the stories—something for characters to do with their hands—or in what specific situations drinking (and perhaps smoking) are used to ease potentially awkward social situations. The relationship between plot tensions or crises also needs to be explored more fully, as do relationships between sex, smoking, violence, and drinking. In essence, new research has to go beyond counting and get to the dynamics of presentation: who is involved, why are they involved, and what are the outcomes of specific alcohol, sex, or other health-related scenes.

The most obvious lack of information, however, is in the area of effects: we know very little about how these images impact upon our behaviors and conceptions about the world. We need to be able to ascertain if the images to which people are continually exposed on television do impact upon their ideas. For example, is exposure to messages that neglect the negative aspects of drinking (the typical television message) related to more positive conceptions about drinking? What about sex? How is exposure to messages stressing the casual nature of sexual relations (found in many television programs) related to conceptions about sex and sexuality? How are adolescents' ideas about sex, sexuality, beauty, and ideal body weight related to what they see on television?

Television viewing is deeply integrated into our lives, and television has become an important socialization factor in today's culture. We know that children and adults get all kinds of information from television, some of it positive and some negative. For example, to drug education, television may be providing messages that drinking is "OK" and almost a "necessary" part of social encounters, while using hard drugs leads to disaster. If culturally sustained health hazards are the new frontier in health promotion and disease prevention, there is a need for greater mobilization of effort and resources in a central sector of that frontier. The first step toward such mobilization is the fuller, broader, and more sustained study of the messages television conveys about health, drinking, drug use, and sex and, most important, a refinement and understanding of the contribution these messages make to the conceptions and behaviors of various groups of viewers.

9

Promoting Health Through Entertainment Television

KATHRYN C. MONTGOMERY

One night in March 1989, viewers of ABC's situation comedy, *Who's the Boss*, became the unwitting targets of "message television." One of the show's main characters, 17-year-old Sam, was geting a lecture from her father after she got drunk with her friends at a party. "The bottom line," he warns her, "is I don't want you drinkin'. It's illegal and it's dangerous. . . . This peer pressure stuff is baloney."

This program is one of the many recent instances when prime-time television was used as a vehicle for health promotion. In this case, the show was a "dedicated episode," where an entire show was devoted to the prosocial message. It was part of a major campaign by Harvard University's School of Public Health to use entertainment TV to warn people about the dangers of alcohol abuse and drunk driving.

Public health issues are not new to entertainment television. They have become staples of prime-time as well as daytime programming. Some of them appear because of the efforts of health advocacy organizations. Others find their way to television screens through writers and producers who are constantly looking for topical material. Major diseases have spawned dozens of "disease-of-the-week" TV movies—from newscaster Betsy Rollin's own story about breast cancer in *First*

AUTHOR'S NOTE: My graduate students Wendy Colman, Janice Drickey, Mary Herczog, and Potter Palmer contributed some of the research for this chapter. I am grateful for their input. I would also like to thank Peter Broderick for his help in editing the manuscript.

114

You Cry (CBS, 1978), to a family's struggle with AIDS in *An Early Frost* (NBC, 1985); to the heartbreak of herpes in *Intimate Agony* (ABC, 1983). Other health issues—such as drug abuse, birth control, and smoking—have been peppered throughout episodic TV.
How effectively has entertainment television promoted public health? Most scholars have addressed this question by analyzing the content of prime-time and daytime programs. There is a large body of content analysis research examining television's depictions of such topics as health and illness, alcohol consumption, and food and nutrition (see Signorielli, Chapter 8). This chapter focuses on the forces outside and inside the television industry that play a role in selecting and shaping images and issues related to public health. What are the imperatives and constraints that influence the way health-related issues are treated? What can entertainment TV do well in this area, and where is it lacking?

Much of the information summarized in this chapter comes from the author's six-year study of the relationship between advocacy groups and prime-time network television (Montgomery, 1989). Also included are the results of a recent research project on the depiction of AIDS on TV. These studies are part of a small but growing body of scholarship examining institutional processes in entertainment television (Cantor, 1979, 1980; Gitlin, 1979, 1983; Montgomery, 1981, 1989; Newcomb, 1983; Pekurny, 1982; Turow, 1984, 1985, 1989).

In some ways, entertainment TV appears to be the perfect vehicle for the promotion of public health. It is at the center of mainstream cultural activity, reaching large portions of the American public with a constant stream of programming. As a popular art form, it has a unique ability to engage viewers in ways that news and public affairs programs do not. For young people, it serves as an "electronic classroom," where lessons are taught each week through the actions of its characters.

Entertainment programming also plays an increasingly important role as a forum for the presentation of major public issues. Television draws more and more of its program ideas from the news media, refashioning these topical "headline" stories into TV movies and series episodes. As "infotainment" programs proliferate and television movies gradually replace network documentaries, Americans are getting more and more of their information about the important issues of the day from television's unique blending of fact and fiction (see Wallack, Chapters 2 and 11). These developments might provide new opportunities for public health promotion.

But while entertainment television may be in a uniquely powerful position to promote positive attitudes about public health, it also has serious limitations rooted in the very structure of American broadcasting. The fundamental conflict is between TV programming's role as a conveyor of information and its essential function as an "environment" for commercial messages. The ways market forces have shaped the presentation of public health information in entertainment television are illustrated in the following cases.

HOLLYWOOD LOBBYISTS

Since the 1970s, a number of social issue groups have approached the creative community to encourage Hollywood writers and producers to incorporate certain issues into entertainment programming. Though the styles of these "Hollywood lobbyists" have varied, they have shared a common set of strategies and tactics for working with the entertainment industry. They have approached industry personnel in a cooperative rather than a confrontational manner—making suggestions to the creative community, providing valuable resource materials, and maintaining cordial relations with key producers and writers, as well as giving occasional input on scripts and story ideas when requested. They have used various techniques to create a climate of awareness about their issues and to "sensitize" members of the television industry. Several groups have formed alliances with particularly influential producers (Montgomery, 1989).

The most successful groups have been those with issues and goals "compatible" with the needs of entertainment programming. These issues lend themselves well to dramatic treatment, or they can easily be incorporated into the background of entertainment programs—what Gerbner and Gross refer to as the "backdrop of reality" in the "world of television" (Gerbner & Gross, 1976).

SUBSTANCE ABUSE

The issue of alcohol abuse has proven to be quite compatible with the needs of entertainment programming. The topic of alcoholism is inherently dramatic. The case histories of drug addicts and alcoholics have provided story lines for entertainment media for years: in theatrical films like *The Lost Weekend* and *The Days of Wine and Roses*, as well as in countless soap operas and prime-time dramas (Cook & Lewington, 1979). Alcohol-related subject matter is also easily woven into the background of entertainment television. And the issue is fairly noncontroversial, since no one openly favors alcohol abuse.

Several campaigns have focused on alcohol abuse in entertainment television. Warren Breed and James De Foe, with funding from the U.S. Public Health Service, set up an office in Los Angeles in the late 1970s to change the portrayal of alcohol consumption in prime time television. They conducted a content analysis of programming, which showed not only that drinking was frequent on TV, but also that the wrong lessons were being taught to viewers. They found, for example, that characters seldom refused a drink and often drank alcohol to face a crisis (Breed & De Foe, 1982).

These findings were presented to the television production community in a series of workshops. By approaching the industry cooperatively and in a nonthreatening manner, the two consultants found a number of producers and writers willing to listen to their suggestions. Breed and De Foe did not ask that drinking be completely removed from prime time. They wanted TV to play an educational role by placing drinking in "an appropriate context so that a realistic picture of alcohol use and abuse could be shown." The team worked in Hollywood for several years. On a few programs, their input was fairly extensive. They worked closely with the producers and writers of *M*A*S*H*, when the show's lead character, Hawkeye, confronted his own problem with alcohol. With other series, the team usually asked only for a "reality reminder," a "word, phrase, or joke that would point out the reality of drinking without causing anyone to step out of character" (Breed & De Foe, 1982, p. 92).

In 1988, the Center for Health Communication at Harvard University's School of Public Health launched a similar campaign, encouraging top executives at the major networks, as well as producers and writers of entertainment programming, to insert messages in their programs about the dangers of drinking and driving. One goal was to promote the idea of the "designated driver."

Leaders of the campaign approached the creative community carefully, making suggestions for possible ways to incorporate these messages into programming without being heavy-handed. After the first year of the campaign (which also included a series of public service announcements), the Harvard program took credit for scenes, dialogue, or entire episodes in more than 25 television programs. The campaign was heavily publicized in the press, as well as on television news and talk shows.

Several other groups have worked with the Hollywood creative community around alcohol and drug issues. The Scott Newman Center was founded by actor Paul Newman during the late 1970s in memory of his son who died of a drug overdose. Since that time, it has worked with the Hollywood community to encourage television to deal responsibly with both drug and alcohol abuse. The organization gives yearly awards for excellence in dealing with substance issues in the media. The American Cancer Society recently completed a two-year program in Hollywood designed to reduce smoking by TV characters and to encourage anti-smoking scenes and dialogue.

The groups working with Hollywood on alcohol and drug abuse have understood the rules of the game for dealing with the television industry. In addition to maintaining cordial relations with the creative community, these organizations have been careful to limit their expectations and operations to a narrow range of appropriate activities. They have not asked for major changes in programming content, only for minor adjustments that could easily be accommodated. The messages they have sought to incorporate into entertainment television have emphasized personal responsibility and individual behavior. Certain issues have been carefully avoided because they might not be well received by the television industry. For example, these groups have stayed away from more controversial topics such as increasing alcohol excise taxes or restricting alcohol advertising.

Over the years, the television industry has been particularly willing to cooperate with organizations involved with substance abuse. Not only is the issue compatible with programming needs but it also serves to enhance television's image as a socially responsible medium. The incorporation of prosocial messages on drunk driving, drug abuse, and anti-smoking has put network television in a favorable light and has served as an effective buffer to public criticism. In some instances, this programming has also been used to head off efforts to regulate the industry. In 1984, when a coalition of public health groups, spearheaded by the Washington-based Center for Science in the Public Interest, proposed legislation that would ban alcohol advertising from radio and TV, the broadcast industry organized a massive counter campaign that defeated the plan. The campaign included presentation before Congress of excerpts from prime-time programs, featuring anti-alcohol scenes and dialogue.

The television industry considers substance abuse so important that it has launched several initiatives of its own, including the establishment of organizations within the industry to ensure that entertainment programming continues to put forth appropriate prosocial messages. The Caucus for Producers, Writers, and Directors issued a "white paper," in 1982, titled "We've Done Some Thinking . . .," which urged the creative community to treat alcohol-related issues more responsibly. In 1983, an Entertainment Industries Council (EIC) was set up to "deglamorize drug and alcohol use." The EIC has issued periodic guidelines on issues related to alcohol and drug abuse, as well as public safety. For example, a recent memo to creative community members offered these suggestions:

(1) To emphasize that alcohol is a drug, please use phrases such as "the abuse of alcohol and other drugs" rather than "substance abuse."

(2) There is no "recreational" use of illicit drugs. Please refer to all use as "use of illicit drugs."

(3) "Mood altering" drugs tends to be a weak and inaccurate description of the powerful effect that drugs have on the mind. It is recommended that the phrase "mind altering" be used.

(4) The term "workaholic" trivializes the alcohol dependence problem. Please attempt to substitute the phrase "compulsive worker."

The Academy of Television Arts and Sciences has also become involved with alcohol and drug abuse issues. The academy held a "Substance Abuse Conference" in 1986, kicked off by a keynote speech from First Lady Nancy Reagan, and featuring leaders in the public health field and the entertainment industry. A special substance abuse committee was established within the academy to continue urging producers and writers to deglamorize alcohol and other drugs. The committee also serves as a liaison to such outside organizations as the White House Conference for a Drug Free America, the National Council on Alcoholism, and the U.S. Department of Education. White House drug czar William Bennett was invited to address the TV industry in 1989. The academy also coordinated arrangements for an animated substance abuse special directed to children aired simultaneously by ABC, CBS, and NBC in 1990.

The television industry has enthusiastically embraced the substance abuse issue, as long as the demands for change have been clearly circumscribed. By creating its own internal mechanisms for monitoring and controlling the representation of alcohol and drugs, the industry has succeeded in deflecting much of the external criticism directed toward it, while ensuring that the messages in its programming do not conflict with the imperatives of the TV business.

Consequently, most of the television programs that have dealt with the issue have kept the focus on personal behavior, while avoiding the larger external political and social causes of alcohol and drug abuse. A recent content analysis of alcohol in prime-time television noted that the frequency of drinking has gone down (Wallack, Grube, Madden, & Breed, in press). But these researchers doubted whether any substantive changes have occurred in the way entertainment television handled this issue:

> It is less clear, however, that the predominant messages regarding the use of alcohol in society and the most appropriate ways to respond to alcohol problems have changed very much. Drinking is something done by attractive characters with positive attributes. When problems do occur, they are treated at the individual level, factors external to the individual that are important to the prevention and treatment of alcohol problems are seldom addressed, and the community aspects of alcohol issues are rarely explored."

This kind of treatment is consistent with the way entertainment television deals with most social and political issues, a pattern that Gitlin (1983) refers to as the "domestication of social issues." Keeping the focus consistently on what individuals can do creates fewer problems for programmers, networks, and advertisers.

"SENSITIVE" ISSUES

Public health issues that have become highly politicized are particularly problematic for entertainment television. Even when presented as individual concerns, these issues can still pose problems for television. Such is the case with birth control and abortion. Although there have been organized efforts around them for nearly 20 years, these issues have been difficult to introduce into programming. Sexuality and reproductive rights are so politically charged that any reference to them in entertainment programming has generated concern within the industry. The television industry has often had to walk a tightrope between advocacy groups with opposing views on how these issues should be presented.

In the early 1970s, the New York-based Population Institute approached the heads of the three networks, as well as the top producers and writers in the industry, to encourage the incorporation of population control issues into entertainment programs. The idea was to enlist the support of the creators of TV programs in a campaign to raise public awareness about the dangers of overpopulation, an issue that had already become a matter of public concern. The Population Institute conducted a series of seminars and offered cash awards for the best scripts dealing with population control as an incentive to the creative community.

These efforts immediately sparked controversy. The most notorious case involved an episode in 1972 of CBS's *Maude*, in which the 47-year-old lead character accidentally became pregnant and chose to have an abortion. Broadcast only two months before the landmark Supreme Court *Roe v. Wade* decision, the program was attacked by leaders of the Catholic church who accused CBS and producer Norman Lear of using prime time for propaganda purposes. The Population Institute was also targeted for attack and charged with wielding undue influence in Hollywood. Anti-abortion protesters staged a sit-in at network headquarters and organized a letter-writing campaign, pressuring affiliate stations and threatening to boycott the show's sponsors. Though the protesting groups failed to keep the controversial episode from being rebroadcast, they did succeed in stirring up a public debate in the press, causing all advertisers to drop out of the rerun and influencing one-quarter of the network affiliates not to air the show a second time.

Birth Control

Because of their sensitive nature, issues related to sexuality have required special handling in entertainment television. Advocacy groups have had mixed success in convincing the TV industry to deal with these issues. Though programmers have been all too eager to use sex as a way to attract viewers, they have not been so willing to have their characters openly discuss and use birth control. For example, in 1977, NBC programming executives were excited about having the lead character of its popular series, *James at 15*, lose his virginity on his 16th birthday. But when the writer insisted on an oblique reference to birth control in the script, the network refused, fearing reprisals from conservative religious groups and angry parents. As a result, the writer resigned from the series in a cloud of public controversy.

In recent years, advocacy groups have been more successful at getting birth control issues into programming, though it remains a challenging task. Since 1980, the Center for Population Options (CPO) has continued the Hollywood work begun by the Population Institute (which began focusing its efforts elsewhere). CPO worked closely with the Hollywood creative community, offering input on scripts as well as yearly awards for responsible treatment of sexual issues in programming. Due in part to CPO's efforts, by the mid-1980s TV characters were more openly discussing birth control on such popular network series as *Valerie*, *Cagney & Lacey*, and *St. Elsewhere*. But fears of offending certain religious groups continued to make the networks wary. In one case, the producer and writers wanted characters to refer to four types of birth control devices, but the network standards and practices department insisted that only two be mentioned. The networks became more open to including references to birth control when the AIDS crisis became a matter of public concern. As the condom was transformed from a mere contraceptive tool to a life-saving device, mention of it was no longer taboo.

Abortion

Abortion, on the other hand, has remained a divisive and explosive issue in the years following the *Maude* controversy. It has been incorporated into programming very infrequently. In those instances where the issue has been woven into the story line, it has been handled with extreme care, and presented in a "balanced" way. Following a well-entrenched formula for handling such issues, the networks have been careful to include clear expressions of an anti-abortion point of view in each of these programs. Even with this special handling, the abortion issue has continued to cause problems when it has appeared in prime time. A 1985 *Cagney & Lacey* episode about the bombing of an abortion clinic provoked a series of protests by the National Right To Life Committee. Protests also erupted over more recent programs, including a three-part episode on abortion in the CBS series *TV 101* in 1989, and an NBC movie that same year chronicling the events leading up to the historic *Roe v. Wade* decision.

A set of policies and conventions has evolved within the television industry that determines how all issues are treated in entertainment programming. Some of these policies—such as balance—are clearly articulated, consciously invoked rules. Others are less explicit, having become so internalized that they are seldom even discussed. Yet whether explicit or implicit, these policies and conventions have been consistently applied, producing identifiable patterns in prime time.

AIDS

The best recent illustration of how these conventions work is television's handling of the AIDS issue. In a project recently conducted by the author and four graduate students at UCLA, the research focused on those entertainment programs where AIDS was a principal part of the story line. Fourteen such programs were identified between 1985 and 1988 on the NBC, CBS, ABC, and Fox networks. The content of these programs was reviewed, using qualitative analysis. Interviews were then conducted with key decision makers in the production and writing of these programs to find out what considerations were involved in the treatment of this issue. To supplement these interviews, the scripts, network memos, and other written documents were reviewed.

While several organizations have offered suggestions and advice to producers and writers who choose to deal with AIDS, no single advocacy organization has focused its efforts exclusively on encouraging or influencing the incorporation of this issue into programming. Following the common practice in Hollywood, medical experts were consulted on all the programs that included AIDS story lines. But while great care was taken to ensure that each program was fair and accurate in its portrayal of this disease, the cumulative picture of AIDS in network entertainment programming was highly distorted.

The most significant distortion was in the representation of who got AIDS. In the world of entertainment television, the overwhelming majority of people with AIDS were women and children, accounting for more than 75% of the characters with the disease. Only about one-fourth of the TV characters with AIDS were gay men. This was in sharp contrast to the distribution of AIDS in the real world, where gay men make up the overwhelming proportion of people with AIDS. In a number of instances, there was a conscious decision not to have a gay character because of fear that it would only reinforce negative public opinion and perpetuate the notion that AIDS was a "gay disease." But there were also more pragmatic reasons for this choice, which were consistent with prevailing conventions in network television. It was clear in several cases, for example, that the entire issue of homosexuality was purposefully avoided because of its controversial nature. Network executives and producers shied away from dealing with the topic for fear of antagonizing conservative groups or gay activists.

The extremely sensitive nature of this issue is evident in the development of the first serious dramatic treatment of AIDS, NBC's *An Early Frost*, which aired in 1985. The story, which did depict a gay person with the disease, was in development for a very long time before it was finally completed. Throughout the process, the network standards and practices department carefully monitored every line of dialogue, issuing a number of directives designed to carefully frame the presentation of homosexuality, "balancing" it with explicit lines of dialogue from characters openly opposed to the gay life style. "The depiction of the issue of homosexuality," explained one memo, "which is the underlying if not primary theme of the film, should be dealt with in a thoroughly balanced manner. It should be treated factually not ideologically, 'warts and all' but without moral judgments." In another memo, the following instructions were given: "The show should avoid proselytizing either on behalf of or against the homosexual life-style."

When *An Early Frost* was still in the script stage, it had to be approved by the network sales department, which made its own demands on the movie. "The final product," explained one memo, "can be positioned and sold to the advertising community as a story of how a family deals with a crisis, and not perceived as another movie about homosexuals." Careful consideration was given to insulating the commercials, to the extent that special separators were inserted between the programming and ads: "Scenes prior to commercial breaks should avoid being perceived as controversial (i.e., the initial hugging of Michael and Peter at the end of the first act). Show bumpers should be added for commercial protection."

Given these intrusive procedures, it is little wonder that most producers and writers chose to avoid association of AIDS with homosexuality. They were also influenced by a prevailing belief that women and children were inherently more sympathetic characters, making it easier for most TV viewers to identify with them. In several cases where gay characters were shown with the disease, there was a conscious attempt not to let the audience get too close to them. As one writer put it: "We could not develop a character that was so gay that people were going to change the channel." The drama instead focused on reactions of the heterosexual characters, a consistent pattern in entertainment television's treatment of homosexuality (Montgomery, 1981, 1989).

While the highly topical nature of the AIDS issue was attractive to the makers of network entertainment television as a way to draw audiences, efforts were made not only to avoid association with homosexuality but to deemphasize the relationship between sexual behavior and AIDS. One result of this was that in the world of entertainment television, blood transfusions were repeatedly chosen as a cause for the disease, accounting for more than one-third of the TV AIDS cases, while in the real world the figure at the time was less than 5%. Discussions about sexual transmission of AIDS were rare and generally restricted to brief, clinical, obligatory explanations that often stood out noticeably from the story.

Generic considerations also shaped the way the AIDS issue was treated. In several instances the story was almost identical in different programs within the same genre, and it often seemed as if the disease had simply been plugged into a formula. For example, two afterschool specials—*Just a Regular Kid* (ABC) and *An Enemy Among Us* (CBS)—both dealt with teenaged boys exposed to AIDS through a blood transfusion facing social stigma and ostracism at school.

There were also consistent patterns in daytime soaps. Because of their high female viewerships, such programs as *Another World*, *All My Children*, and *The Young and the Restless* consciously chose to introduce the AIDS topic by having a female character contract the disease. In one soap, for example, a special character was created who became ill with the disease and died within a few months of its onset. To avoid disturbing viewers too much by forcing them to witness the ravages of the disease on this glamorous young woman, the producers chose to have her die offscreen while away on a trip to Italy. During her brief stay on the long-running serial, great care was taken to make sure that viewers knew the character was a virgin who had gotten AIDS through a blood transfusion. She was also never allowed to have sexual relations, even though she was romantically involved with a young man (the producers also felt this added to the sexual tension of the story). When one of the show's producers was asked why a special character had to be invented, rather than having one of the show's regulars contract the disease, she seemed surprised at the question. "Are you kidding?" she answered, "with the sexual histories of our characters, all of Bay City would get AIDS!"

Finally, there were significant omissions in TV's portrayal of AIDS. In the programs studied, IV drug users were not among the victims of the disease, nor were poor people or people of color.

DISCUSSION

More research should be conducted to fully understand entertainment television's role in promoting or hindering public health. TV presentation of other health-related issues should be closely examined. More research also should be done on the impact of these messages on viewers, such as Colman's (1990) study of a TV movie's effects on health beliefs.

Some preliminary assessments can be made about how well entertainment television promotes public health. It seems fairly clear that entertainment programming can play an important agenda-setting role, making the public aware of certain public health problems. However, it is only one of many media sources for such information, and it quite often follows print and broadcast news media in its presentation of such issues. For example, AIDS did not begin to appear in entertainment programs until it had been widely reported in the news media.

Entertainment media may also be able to reach audiences that are not as likely to pay attention to news media. Though teenagers watch less television than other population groups, popular prime-time shows may still be effective ways to get their attention on certain issues.

Through repeated messages in both the foreground and background of programs, entertainment TV can depict certain healthy behaviors as normative, and by doing this, may be able to play a role in prevention. If TV characters routinely decline alcoholic beverages, viewers may be inclined to accept such behavior as the appropriate thing to do in their own lives. The virtual absence of cigarette smoking in prime time, combined with the disappearance of cigarette advertising from TV, may have contributed to the dramatic decline in smoking in the United States over the last two decades. It should be noted that important factors such as major anti-smoking campaigns in other media need to be taken into account in explaining the declining smoking rates.

Entertainment programming may play a role in encouraging more understanding and compassion for those suffering from disease. Certain programming genres may be particularly suited to this role. The increasing number of prime-time series with continuing story lines for example, offer opportunities for more realistic presentation of alcoholism, drug abuse, AIDS, and other illnesses. For example, the CBS series *Cagney & Lacey* introduced a story line where one of the show's lead characters, Christine Cagney, struggles with her alcoholism, refusing for a long time to believe she has a problem, and going through a number of experiences before realizing she needs help. Even after she seeks help through Alcoholics Anonymous, she faces continuing challenges in her commitment to stop drinking.

But while entertainment television is no doubt making some contributions to public health awareness, there are certain areas where it is either undermining its own positive efforts or doing an actual disservice. The imperatives and constraints of entertainment TV have produced significant distortions and omissions in the presentation of health issues. Because it is "promotable" and easily dramatized, disease is a frequent presence in daytime and prime-time programming, with the emphasis on acute rather than chronic illnesses (Turow & Coe, 1985; Turow, 1989; Gerbner et al., 1981, 1982). As the study of AIDS shows, entertainment television has difficulty with complicated or controversial health issues, tending to oversimplify or distort them. And entertainment programs consistently reduce social issues—including those related to public health—to personal problems. The repeated messages of entertainment television shift the responsibility for solving public health problems from the society to the individual.

Entertainment television also has a tendency to "use up" issues. While television producers are often quite willing to incorporate topical and prosocial material into their programs, they are rarely inclined to continue dealing with the issue after initial interest has diminished. Instead, they will seek out the next hot topic to draw audiences.

On some health issues, television gives double messages. The prosocial scenes and dialogue in the programs are often in conflict with the carefully crafted commercials that punctuate the programming with increasing frequency. So, while characters in popular sitcoms warn each other, from time to time, about the dangers of drinking, slick ads in other parts of the schedule repeatedly drive home the message that beer and wine are essential to the good life. Similarly, on children's television occasional public service announcements urging youngsters to eat fruit and vegetables are drowned out by a flood of high-powered ads pushing fast foods, candy, and sugar-coated cereals. Such conflicting messages raise serious questions about whether a medium whose primary goal is to promote consumption can really be an effective advocate for public health.

Even with these limitations, entertainment television must not be overlooked as an important source of health information for the American public. And current trends within the industry may shift more of this responsibility away from other media toward entertainment. Federal deregulation of broadcasting has resulted in a sharp decline in public service announcements, forcing health advocates to use other media to promote their messages. And with an increasing interest in public health issues in the news media, these issues should continue to be a marketable commodity that entertainment television can use to increase its audience ratings while enhancing its public image. If professionals in the public health field can understand and accept entertainment television's strengths and limitations, it can be a powerful ally in the effort to promote public awareness about health issues.

10

Effective Mass Communication Strategies for Health Campaigns

BRIAN R. FLAY
DEE BURTON

This chapter examines the conditions under which mass media health campaigns achieve the greatest impact on the public. It is based on a distillation of a large body of scientific research and theory from the mass communication, social psychology, and public health fields. While the thrust of the review is empirical, several of the issues addressed have implications of a philosophical nature that may raise some new questions as well as answering some. Most of the philosophical issues relate to the concern that mass communication messages primarily seek to change individuals, when many public health problems are more appropriately viewed as properties of larger social and political systems rather than individuals (see Wallack, Chapters 2 and 11). This conundrum should be kept in mind as the practical generalizations about individual-level campaign effects are presented.

WHAT IS A CAMPAIGN?

There are numerous definitions of campaigns (Rogers & Storey, 1987), often building on standard dictionary definitions that refer to a

AUTHORS' NOTE: Preparation of this chapter was supported by grants from the National Institute on Drug Abuse, the National Cancer Institute, and the Office for Substance Abuse Prevention.

series of operations in a war. Applied to public health, communication campaigns can be defined as an *integrated* series of communication activities, using *multiple operations and channels*, aimed at populations or *large target audiences*, usually of *long duration*, with a clear *purpose*.

An *integrated* set of activities ideally implies preplanning and organization. In practice, some campaigns that are not extensively preplanned and well coordinated may nevertheless turn out to be well integrated; for example, the antismoking movement has successfully combined campaign efforts from disparate quarters. Nevertheless, many campaigns have failed because of a lack of preplanning and coordination. Clearly, it is advantageous to carefully formulate a plan and to arrange cooperation among various agencies and groups conducting campaigns in specific health domains.

Use of *multiple operations and channels* suggests that a campaign may consist of more than mass communication activities, such as grassroots organizing, activism and confrontation, legislative testimony, and community organization. This chapter is restricted to mass media campaigns, stressing television, while acknowledging the important role of supplemental activities (Lazarsfeld & Merton, 1948).

While the whole population of a country may be targeted, the concept of *large target audiences* typically means specific, well-defined subgroups such as youth, pregnant women, or Mexican-Americans.

Long duration implies that years, rather than months or weeks, are required to achieve maximum effects. Most wars continue for a period of several years, and a sustained effort is needed for warlike health campaigns against smoking, cancer, and drugs.

Purposeful means that the campaign should follow a strategic plan with clear and measurable objectives. Communication campaigns aim to bring about change by influencing either the opinions and behaviors of individuals or, less often, the marketing behavior of corporate heads or the legislative decisions of congressional representatives.

These characteristics of campaigns incorporate all components of definitions proposed by various communication scholars (Atkin, 1981; Paisley, 1981; Rogers & Storey, 1987; Solomon, 1982). These characteristics also define campaigns to market products. Yet, there are distinct differences between commercial advertising and public health campaigns as they are normally designed.

PUBLIC HEALTH CAMPAIGNS VERSUS PRODUCT MARKETING CAMPAIGNS

While there are many similarities, campaigns promoting products differ from health campaigns on the following dimensions (adapted from McCron & Budd, 1981):

Type of change expected. Many health campaigns aim to change fundamental behaviors, whereas most product advertising aims to mobilize an existing predisposition, as in switching brands. Of course, some advertising does seek to create new markets.

Amount of change expected. Health campaigns aim to change a large proportion of the population, and often in large ways. Product advertising campaigners are usually satisfied with small shifts in market share.

Time frame of promised benefits. Health campaigns usually ask their target audience to wait for delayed statistical probabilities, such as reduced likelihood of eventual illness or a few additional years of life. Product advertisers promise immediate certainty and satisfaction.

Presentation of the product. Advertisers can dress up their product in an exaggerated fashion, for a certain amount of deception (e.g., imagery advertising associating social success with buying a particular brand of Scotch) seems to be acceptable to audiences. On the other hand, health campaigners avoid overselling the benefits of a behavior or treatment and the ease of their acquisition.

Available budgets. Commercial advertisers often have massive budgets, while health campaigners usually operate on relatively minuscule monetary resources.

Trustworthiness. People often distrust commercial advertising, even though they may be affected by it. Health campaigns cannot allow distrust to develop, although there appears to be some skepticism of government-sponsored health messages.

Level of evaluation. Advertisers stress formative market research conducted before a campaign. Many health campaigns still ignore evaluation; when research is performed, it tends to be summative evaluation carried out after the campaign.

So, while the defining attributes of health campaigning and product marketing may be the same, the expectations and conditions differ markedly. Indeed, advertising meets the basic defining characteristics of a campaign more closely than do most public health campaigns. In order to attain greater effectiveness, health campaigners must also strive to meet these defining characteristics. Moreover, public health campaigns also need to meet even more basic conditions, as outlined in the remaining sections of this chapter.

NECESSARY CONDITIONS FOR EFFECTIVE CAMPAIGNS

A short sequence of steps, simple to spell out but difficult to accomplish in practice, must be followed for public health campaigns to be maximally effective. The seven steps are (1) develop and use high quality messages, sources, and channels; (2) disseminate to the target audience; (3) gain and keep the attention of the audience; (4) encourage favorable interpersonal communication about the issue; (5) cause changes in behaviors of individuals, along with awareness, knowledge, opinions, attitudes, feelings, normative beliefs, intentions, or skills; (6) cause broader societal changes; (7) obtain knowledge of effects through summative evaluation. In the following sections, we will describe and examine the significance of each condition, noting both the conventional wisdom and contrary views.

Use High-Quality Messages, Sources, and Channels

The message (e.g., "eat less saturated fat") and its source (e.g., the American Heart Association), and the channel used to distribute it (e.g., television) must be acceptable to the target audience and effective at influencing them. Only influential messages from believable sources will change people or society, regardless of how many people are reached on how many occasions.

On the other hand, some believe that the message is irrelevant because the overall social system/environment is a much larger determinant of individual attitudes and behaviors than is a single campaign. From this perspective, what matters is simply that people hear that alternative viewpoints exist. While there may be some truth to this point, particularly if having an alternative view leads to policy debate (see interpersonal communication, below), planned campaigns can increase the probability that such interpersonal communication will be supportive of public health and that some individuals will possibly be helped in making immediate improvements in their health behavior.

Determinants of achieving high-quality messages, sources, and channels fall into three major areas: needs assessment, application of theory, and formative research.

Needs assessment. In order to develop better messages, the campaign planner should gain more knowledge about the problem they are addressing, the target audience, and the relevant social issues.

Campaigners must know as much as they possibly can about the *problem* that their campaign will address, its prevalence in various subgroups of society, and its biological and social causes and correlates. Without such information, they are unable to effectively address the issue. Campaign planners must know their *target audience*: the salience of the issue to them, their involvement in it, and where they are cognitively, affectively, and behaviorally (Bauer, 1964; Flay & Cook, 1981, 1989; Cartwright, 1949).

In addition, planners must know the relevant *societal conditions* surrounding the issue and social attitudes toward it, including the awareness level of politicians, the media, the population, special interest groups, minorities, and their likely acceptance/support of a campaign. For example, almost any antismoking campaign might be more effective with adults today than an anti-alcohol campaign because of the stronger norms against smoking.

Application of theory. Theory from social psychology can inform message content and structure (Bandura, 1977, 1978, 1986; Fishbein & Ajzen, 1975; Flay, 1981; McGuire, 1984, 1985), channel selection (Katz, 1980), knowledge of the target audience (Bauer, 1964; Blumler & Katz, 1974), and the general structure of the campaign (Flay, 1981). See Flay (1981) and Flay, d'Avernas, Best, Kersell, and Ryan (1983) for attempts to integrate these theories. The key theoretical concepts are highlighted in italics throughout the remainder of the chapter.

Formative research. The development of ideas and concepts for a campaign should be informed by needs assessment, often included as part of formative research. Concepts and preproduction messages should be pretested with samples of the target audience before final production. Special care is needed to avoid unintended effects or unintended meanings—e.g., the "smoking fetus" PSA, intended to motivate pregnant women to quit smoking, aroused the ire of pro-choice advocates regarding abortion because it portrayed a fetus as a fully formed human being. Formative research will often lead to changes in message content or form (Flay, 1987a; Flay, Kessler, & Utts, 1989; Palmer, 1981; Worden et al., 1989).

Disseminate the Messages Well

To be effective, a message must *reach* the target audience, be *repeated frequently* (up to certain limits) and *consistently* but with some *novelty*, for long periods of time (*duration*). Product advertising often meets all of these conditions, but health campaigns rarely do. The North Karelia and Stanford Heart Disease Prevention projects (Maccoby & Solomon, 1981; McAlister, Puska, & Salonen, 1982) are planned campaigns that were effective due to extensive dissemination of messages.

It is worth remembering, however, that good dissemination will be wasted on poor messages. Also, dissemination will increase "spontaneously," through opinion leaders and interpersonal discussion, if the message is "good."

There are five important mediators of effective message dissemination: media gatekeepers, political and social support, financial support, target audience characteristics, and message characteristics.

Media gatekeepers. People and corporations in control of media channels determine what can be aired or printed, the amount and type of coverage, and its timeliness and duration. Campaign planners should know their media gatekeepers' interests and potential conflicts of interest. They must also remember the *agenda-setting* functions of the media (Gandy, 1982; McCombs & Shaw, 1972). They might consider how news on the campaign topic is handled by the proposed channel, and whether news writers feel compelled to obtain an opposing point of view or not (and if so, whether this works to the advantage or disadvantage of the campaign). The type of message developed for telecast will certainly be different in cases where a countermessage can be expected, than in cases where the message will be delivered unchallenged.

Another consideration is whether conflicting interests lead to censorship; certain magazines may be restricted in what smoking or drinking stories they will carry because of their cigarettes or alcohol advertisers (see Wallack, Chapters 2 and 11; Meyer, Chapter 3; Klaidman, Chapter 4; and reviews and analyses by Minkler, Wallack, and Madden, 1987, Warner, 1985, and Whalen, Sheridan, Meister, & Mosher, 1981).

Finally, there is the issue of conflicting interests possibly leading to a lack of credibility. For example, is the Advertising Council a credible agency to sponsor an alcohol reduction campaign? Arguments may be made in either direction on this issue, but the important factor is what the target audience believes.

Political and social support. The more support a campaign has from other sources, the easier it will be to get a new message disseminated. Opposition to the campaign message position makes the task more difficult. Therefore, *supplementing* an ongoing campaign (e.g., anti-smoking, drug abuse prevention, or AIDS education) might be more easily achieved, up to certain limits, than starting a campaign on a new issue. Entering a controversial area, such as pregnancy prevention, might be more difficult.

Financial support. Extensive financial support may help remove political and social barriers, though it does not guarantee it. Financial support will also enable the purchase of desirable time, rather than relying on donations of undesirable time (e.g., Bauman, Brown, Fisher, Padgett, & Sweeney, 1989; Worden et al., 1989).

Target audience characteristics. Is the target audience of interest to the chosen media channel? Does the target audience use the chosen channel? When exposure is voluntary, the best predictor of whether or not the target audience will be exposed to the message or campaign is their normal, everyday media-use habits.

Are there knowledge and health gaps where those most in need are least likely to be reached or are less likely to comprehend the message, or to act on it? Campaign planners should try to reduce such gaps by segmenting the target audience and making extra efforts to reach those most in need with appropriately tailored messages.

Will the message appeal to the target audience? Will it attract new viewers, listeners, or readers to the channel, or at least not turn loyal audiences away? Since most U.S media are funded by advertisers rather than directly supported by the audiences, such audience responses may be important.

Can the target audience be "captured" in some way? An example would be by requiring viewing of a televised series as homework for a coordinated school-based program (Flay et al., 1987, 1988). Campaign planners might think about the use of "penny media" (e.g., posters, flyers, leaflets) in other situations where audiences can be captured.

Message characteristics. The content of the message and the quality of its production will be considered by media gatekeepers. The content cannot be too controversial for most gatekeepers, nor be seen as possibly evoking other controversial issues (e.g., again, the ill-fated "smoking fetus" PSA). The message must appear to gatekeepers to appeal to regular audiences. Large programs or series must not only appeal to but hopefully also increase the audience. Production quality must be similar to other material used by the chosen channel.

Attract the Attention of the Target Audience

The third major requirement for a successful campaign is that the target audience must be exposed to it (that is, to see, hear, or read the message), attend to it, process it, and remember it. This is a generalization that may be challenged. Indeed, mere exposure may sometimes be sufficient to cause attitude and behavior change without knowledge change or even much awareness (see *order of effects* below for more on these alternative points of view).

Gaining the attention of the target audience depends on the characteristics of the receivers, the message, and the channel; attention is also determined by the match between messages and audience, and by the level and type of interpersonal communication stimulated by the message.

Target audience characteristics. Education level, salience of the issue, involvement in the issue, and access to the media channels used are all important. Demographic variables, commonly the only audience characteristics considered, are helpful in selecting the broad channel, such as radio for adolescents. However, a more detailed profile is necessary to select placement or time. Campaign planners must anticipate possibly selective exposure and perception, as individuals may choose to ignore or derogate the message, the source, or the channel. Strategists might attempt to "capture" the audience instead.

Planners should also consider the changing values of the target group. For example, during the last decade, Americans have become less concerned with security and self-fulfillment and more concerned with a sense of accomplishment and with warm relationships with others (Kahle, Poulous, & Sukhdial, 1988). Product marketers keep track of shifts in values; health campaigners must do the same.

Message characteristics. Messages may be rational or emotional, educational or persuasive, action-oriented or not, one-sided or two-sided, fear-eliciting or not, etc. (see McGuire, 1985, for a detailed review of these considerations). It is generally believed that informational messages are better than emotional ones, though eliciting empathy is almost always desirable. Use of fear is good for many health issues, as long as the audience is given a constructive way of reducing the fear. Action messages are usually good in that they get the audience closer to the desired behavior. There may be some cases, however, where action messages seem less credible than purely informational ones. For instance, in Beltramini's (1988) analysis of perceived believability of health warning labels on cigarette packages, he found that specifying the consequences of smoking led to stronger believability than suggesting risk-reducing behaviors.

Messages need to be simple, without being reductionistic. The most profound and complex events and issues can be communicated simply and concisely once they are understood. It is possible that public health professionals have become overinvested in individual life-style factors in disease and mortality reduction due to a lack of adequate understanding of social and economic forces. It is often productive to disturb the cognitive equilibrium of the target audience, thus provoking thought. This is an anti-narcotizing principle.

Morley and Walker (1987) found that novelty, importance, and plausibility must go together—that dropping one of these three attributes significantly reduces the power of the message. Pierce, Dwyer, Frape, Chapman, Chamberlain, and Burke (1986), in a study of smoking cessation, found that health belief content by itself was not effective, and that social influence content by itself was counterproductive, but that both together were powerful.

Channel characteristics. Campaign messages must appear in channels used by the target audience, at the times or in the shows that they watch or listen to. Knowing that pregnant smokers watch television a great deal is not sufficient; planners need to know what and when they watch.

Match of target audience and message positions. Cartwright's (1949) concept of *canalization* suggests the strategy of moving the target audience only a small step at a time. Audiences must see any advocated action as meeting an existing goal. For example, televised "quit smoking" clinics probably would not have been effective in the 1950s, because not enough people knew about the dangers of smoking or were motivated to quit. Today, the emphasis should be on behavior change programs, with only enough awareness and motivation programs to keep the issue on people's minds and to keep them informed (and to reach "confirmed smokers" who might need special motivational attention).

Interpersonal communication. The more people discuss the issue, the more likely they are to attend to the message. Conversely, the more the campaigns can get people to pay attention to the messages, the more likely those people are to engage in future interpersonal discussion about the issue.

Encourage Interpersonal Communication

The fourth major requirement for a meaningful campaign is to increase favorable discussion about the issue. This can be particularly useful if it leads to debate of policy alternatives. The point is that the more people talk about (and therefore also think about) an issue, the greater are the chances of change. Of course, unfavorable discussion may sometimes lead to greater commitment to prior positions. To avoid this, campaign planners need to monitor public attitudes and modify their approach and messages accordingly.

The probability of favorable interpersonal communication depends on the target audience, message, source, and channel characteristics, and the level of attention paid to the message by the target audience.

Target audience characteristics. Two aspects of audience predispositions are relevant: involvement in the issue and readiness for change. More involved audience members, especially those contemplating change, are more likely to discuss the issue with others. The campaign, or some messages, may need to focus on increasing involvement or motivating people to contemplate change. In the field of smoking cessation, the work of Prochaska and DiClemente (1983) provides a frame of reference for developing messages for smokers at various levels of readiness for change. The Stanford Three Community researchers (Maccoby & Solomon, 1981; McAlister, Puska, Salonen, 1982) were also sensitive to this issue. They used Cartwright's (1949) *levels of change* model as the guiding framework.

The involvement of opinion leaders is another important factor. Research on the *diffusion of innovations* (Rogers & Shoemaker, 1971) suggests that enlisting respected leaders in the campaign cause and having them involved in interpersonal interactions with groups of the target audience will be helpful. Campaign implementers might also set up *supplementary* face-to-face viewing and discussion groups, or even clinics for weight loss.

Message, source, channel characteristics. Five promising strategies can improve the interpersonal communication climate: increasing salience, promoting debate, monopolizing the issue, supplementing the media messages, and using the media to supplement other efforts.

If the campaign issue is not salient to members of the target audience, salience should be increased by appealing to the audience's needs and values. Level of controversy of the campaign issue is also important; it may be possible to make the issue, or some aspect of it, controversial enough to promote debate about policy alternatives. This may be especially useful if the social trends are moving in the right direction. Controversy can backfire, however, if it motivates media gatekeepers to reject a campaign, as discussed above.

Attempting to *monopolize* the issue is unlikely for most health issues. Indeed, many health messages are contradicted or amended by the opposite viewpoint presented editorially or by advertising. But *breaking an existing near-monopoly* may be almost as useful, for it leads to a more balanced presentation of information to target audiences. This is one reason the FCC-mandated antismoking counteradvertising of 1968-1970 was effective (Warner, 1981; Flay, 1987b, 1987c).

Community, school, worksite, or clinic components might *supplement media* activities. Campaign planners might also attempt to increase social support for the issue and individuals who attempt change. For example, in the smoking area, adding written material to accompany a television program has been found to double effectiveness and adding discussion groups triples it (Flay, 1987b, 1987c). The mass media can also be used to *supplement other efforts* on those issues where the media are not the driving force of a campaign, by complementing ongoing interventions of government, industry, schools, and other agencies (Flay, 1986a).

Attention to the message. Just as the target audience must pay attention to a campaign message if they are to be changed by it, maximizing audience attention is also important in generating interpersonal communication. People who attend to the message are more likely to discuss the issue with others. Conversely, involving people in discussion will increase the likelihood of their attending to future messages.

Cause Individual Change

To be judged effective, a mass communications campaign has to change the awareness, knowledge, opinions, attitudes, feelings, normative beliefs, intentions, skills, or behaviors, and ultimately the health, of the target audience. An alternative view is that campaigns can only change knowledge, not attitudes, and certainly not behaviors. Another alternative view is that it is inappropriate or even unethical to focus campaigns on changing individuals. Under either of these alternative assumptions, the major objective should be to change society or the system. There is truth to both points of view, and campaign planners need to work from both perspectives.

Whether a campaign succeeds in changing individuals depends on audience characteristics, their attention to the message, interpersonal communication, and the level of broader social change. This section also examines the conditions necessary for behavioral change, different orders of effects, and the maintenance of changes.

Audience characteristics. Campaign planners should know as much as possible about their target audience. Everything above being equal, certain people will be more readily changed than others. This may be because of personality differences, availability of behavioral alternatives, availability of other resources, or other priorities. Campaign planners should initially target those who are most ready for change, but they also need to target motivational messages to those less ready for change.

Attention. Those who attend to the message are more likely to change in the intended direction than those who do not attend to the message. Campaign planners need to maximize attention to these messages. However, *self-selection* may still operate, such that individuals who are more ready for change may be the first ones, or the only ones, to attend to the message (Zillmann & Bryant, 1985).

Interpersonal communication. Two groups usually discuss issues: those ready for change and those who are committed to their position and wish to convert others to it. By targeting the former group, campaign messages can encourage discussion between these two groups.

Societal change. The more society changes, the more individuals will change. Thus, even campaigns targeted at individual change should attempt to modify the social environment or influence social policy in ways that encourage and reinforce the desired changes once individuals make them. Smoking cessation, for example, is more likely to be sustained if individuals receive support from their spouses or friends; appropriate changes in worksite policy may be even more supportive.

What effects can mass media really bring about? Without doubt, awareness can be raised and knowledge increased by mass communications campaigns. Attitude change and motivation to act differently are harder to accomplish. Substantial behavior change is even more difficult, but not impossible. *Social learning theory* (Bandura, 1977, 1986) and the *health belief model* (Becker, 1974), among other theories, suggest that behavior change can be produced by the following:

(1) Demonstrate or model the desired behavior.

(2) Present the behavior as effective in achieving desirable objectives, particularly immediate ones such as feeling and looking better.

(3) Present the behavior as pertinent to real-life circumstances, rather than in the abstract. Heighten the incentive or value of a particular level of freedom from risk.

(4) Instill the belief that a particular act or pattern of behavior will preclude or ameliorate a specific risk. Nurture the motive to avoid harm or improve well-being in the longer term.

(5) Present the behavior as enjoying the approval and support of the community.

(6) Mobilize public support for the desired changes.

(7) Provide specific guidance for the self-management of behavior change.

(8) Provide specific guidance for the self-management of relapses by recycling and trying again.

(9) Encourage the development of interpersonal social support for change attempts and changed behavior.

(10) Provide the infrastructures to support change attempts and changed behavior, encouraging the use of existing infrastructures, or encouraging proactive behavior by the target audience to apply pressure on government or other responsible agencies to provide such infrastructures.

(11) Encourage activism against any part of the social system that tends to undermine the desired behavioral changes.

It should be noted that many of these suggestions are consistent not only with basic behavior change theory, but also with increasing attention, interpersonal communication, social support, and reinforcement of change.

Order of effects. There are several potential hierarchies of effects for ordering change (Ray, 1973). The most common order, in terms of how professionals usually conceive of the effects of their media messages, is cognitive-affective-conative (behavioral), called the *learning hierarchy*. In other words, knowledge is changed first, then attitudes, and lastly, behaviors (i.e., K-A-B). Although this sequence is usual only for salient issues in which the target audience is highly involved and where the choices are clear-cut and very different, such conditions are common for health issues. However, where salience and involvement is initially low, the campaigner may need to work on increasing it before attempting to change K-A-B.

Another common order is the *low involvement hierarchy*, where people are not involved in the issue and there are minimal differences between alternatives. Most purchasing decisions are of this type, so much product advertising follows this model. The order is cognitive (awareness of a new brand), conative (trial behavior), affective (like or dislike the new product). This order is less often relevant for health issues.

A third common order is the *dissonance-attribution hierarchy*, conative-affective-cognitive. When people are involved in the issue, but the alternatives are almost indistinguishable, they may try something, decide that they like it (attitude), and then selectively attend to information that supports their decision. Alternatively, if people can be forced into a new behavior (e.g., by legislation such as in forced integration), or otherwise "bribed" or tricked into trying something (e.g., by the use of free gifts for visiting a time-share vacation resort), they may decide that they like it and then find the information to support their position. A positive affective reaction to an emotional or associative message might lead to the same chain of effects.

Maintenance of effects. This requires consideration of reinforcements, social support, and systemic support, all of which have been discussed above.

Cause Societal Change

The long-term maintenance of individual-level effects and the ultimate effectiveness of a campaign requires parallel changes in society. Ultimate effects on health status (morbidity and mortality) require behavior changes by the bulk of the target population, not just the 5% to 10% of the population that can be influenced most easily by media campaigns. Thus, a complete campaign must consist of more than mass communications. The media should be *supplemented* by community and government involvement and changes (Rogers & Storey, 1987). Alternatively, the appropriate target individuals for a campaign might sometimes be politicians, so they can start to change the system concurrently with a subsequent campaign targeted to populations.

Whether the target of change is health behavior or voting behavior, ultimately the level of societal change depends on both the kind and amount of individual change and the degree of interpersonal communication.

Individual effects. The accumulation of individuals who have changed leads to changes in social norms which, in turn, lead to societal changes, and can lead to systemic changes.

Interpersonal communication. A campaign targeted to individuals can lead to social changes if enough of those individuals discuss it with others—especially with politicians and other opinion leaders in a position to bring about changes.

Obtain Knowledge of Campaign Effects

A final requirement for campaign effectiveness is accumulation of knowledge about effects and impact. Public health, media, government, and private agency employees should know what has worked, for whom, under what conditions. While such knowledge may not influence the success of an already implemented campaign, it will influence the nature and effectiveness of future campaigns. Future campaigns can be improved only if planners know what worked and why (Flay, 1987b, 1987c). Lack of such knowledge will lead to repeating old mistakes.

An alternative view to this position is that the only important thing is to care about people and to try something. Under this view, evaluation and research are a waste of resources that should be put into public education (the point of view of some voluntary health agencies). Of course, the rebuttal to this alternative view is that with sufficient evaluation, it might be discovered that campaigns are not "doing good" after all, so there is a need to do something different to meet societal goals.

Two mediators of knowledge of effects are the desire to know and the quality level of summative evaluation.

Desire to know. Obviously, without the desire to know, no attempt, or inadequate attempts, will be made to determine the effects of campaigns. Those who subscribe to the "we care and are doing something practical" view might find it against their interests to know. Would the Advertising Council want to know if their anti-alcohol campaign was ineffective in all respects but attaining good public relations for them?

Those who subscribe to the "it's a waste of resources" point of view probably believe—perhaps mistakenly—that they know how to design a campaign and thus do not need to "waste" resources finding out. It might also be against their best interests to find out, for public education is believed to be a good public relations that leads to greater contributions for basic research.

Summative evaluation. Only high-quality summative evaluation can inform campaigners about the effects of a particular campaign. Three broad models of evaluation of single studies and synthesis approach are common (Flay & Cook, 1981, 1989). The *advertising model* focuses on the beginning of the presumed causal chain; it is usually limited to assessing total audience size and recall and recognition of the message. The *impact monitoring model* focuses near the end of the presumed causal chain, using archival data. The use of per capita consumption of tobacco to determine the effects of counteradvertising and publicity is probably the best example of this approach. It is valuable for assessing effects of campaigns of long duration, but not for assessing the effects of normal campaigns or specific components of long ones. The *experimental model* attempts a more comprehensive assessment of effects from different levels of the presumed causal chain, and it also attempts to control for alternative explanations for any observed effects. It is the model most favored by scholars but the one most difficult to implement in the real world. However, the Stanford Heart Disease Prevention Project is a prime example of the approach for long and multifaceted campaigns, and there is a significant number of examples for shorter, more focused programs (Flay, 1981).

In the long term, *synthesis* (or *meta-analysis*) of results from all types of evaluations will be most informative. That is, no single study is definitive for the field, though it may often have to be considered as definitive for a particular issue at a particular time and location. However, no synthesis of value is possible without large numbers of methodologically superior single studies.

CONCLUSIONS: IMPLICATIONS FOR CAMPAIGN DESIGN

In conclusion, seven implications for campaign design can be drawn from this exploration of theory and practice:

(1) It is desirable to meet every one of the conditions discussed; indeed, most of them are necessary. Because so few campaigns have met most of these conditions, few campaigns have been of proven effectiveness.

(2) One clear implication is the need for more research at the front end of campaign design, particularly needs assessment and formative research. Product marketers devote substantial resources to marketing research. In contrast, health campaigners tend to concentrate on evaluating the result, if they conduct any evaluation at all. Health campaigners need to place far greater emphasis on marketing research if they are ever to be successful. Theories and research from social psychology (information processing, attitude change and persuasion, consistency theories), other areas of psychology (social learning theory), public health (the Health Belief Model), sociology and communications research (agenda setting, uses and gratifications, the diffusion and adoption of innovations, the knowledge gap, etc.), and findings from evaluations of past campaigns all provide a firm basis for campaign planning, especially when taken together. The need is for greater focus on the preproduction end of campaign development, including needs assessment, the use of focus groups, concept testing, and other phases of formative research (Flay, 1987a).

(3) Planners should pay greater attention to dissemination. Some potentially effective messages have failed to get exposure and reach their target audience because of failures at this stage. Many potentially effective campaigns have failed because of the common reliance on free PSA space or time, and the resulting lack of control over channel and time placement. Public health agencies and advocates need to make greater use of paid time, public relations (Klein & Danzig, 1985), media advocacy (see Wallack, Chapter 11), and other creative approaches to obtaining exposure (DeJong & Winsten, 1989).

(4) Audience attention, acceptance, and change can be maximized by careful work at all of the earlier steps in production. Successful intervention requires communication that can (a) inform the individual about the potential risks and benefits, particularly those that are immediate and of high probability (and, therefore, most salient), (b) inform the individual of the opportunity to act, (c) provide realistic guidelines for action, and (d) demonstrate that taking action is feasible and will result in the desired outcome. This needs to take place in the context of the audience's current position or development, with carefully planned phases designed to assess changes and build upon them.

(5) Campaign designers should also maximize favorable interpersonal communication about the campaign issue, particularly among members of the target audience. Interpersonal communication about effective messages can contribute to the sense among the public at large that the community supports their position. Targeting other persons important to the target audience (e.g., parents and teachers of adolescents) can help

generate discussion. Public debate can lead to important changes in political agenda and even important policy changes in support of the campaign.

(6) Planners should always aim for both individual and societal level changes, rather than confining themselves to one level or the other. Effective public health education aims directly at both the individual and the norms and values in the individual's social milieu that support the behavior (Leventhal & Cleary, 1980; Lichtenstein & Mermelstein, 1984). Of course, this requires careful implementation of a long-term strategic plan featuring distinct phases (multicomponent), each with realistic, specific, and measurable objectives (Flay, Kessler, & Utts, 1989; DeJong & Winsten, in press).

(7) Some type of summative evaluation should always be conducted so the public health community can learn to do better in the future. Though the current state-of-the-art suggests an emphasis on the need for formative research even more than the need for summative evaluation, it must be stressed that all levels of evaluation and research are necessary in the grander view of things (Flay, 1986b).

If all this sounds like a lot, that's because it is! DeJong and Winsten (1989) provide an equally long and complex set of recommendations for the use of mass media for drug abuse prevention. It is pertinent to recall Paisley's (1981) paraphrase of Winston Churchill: "Mass communication campaigns seem like a noisy and inefficient way to achieve social change—until you consider the alternatives" (p. 40). Current knowledge now gives us the potential to make campaigns much more efficient, if no less noisy!

11

Improving Health Promotion:
Media Advocacy and
Social Marketing Approaches

LAWRENCE WALLACK

The mass media can be a powerful tool for promoting health around the world. There are, however, many complexities associated with optimal use of this powerful resource. Some argue that public communication campaigns can be a source of accurate health information for individuals and that mass media can inform public debate about health issues. The media are perceived to be a valuable and willing partner.

Others argue that the media are a source of "anti-health education," presenting people with inaccurate or misleading health information through advertising, entertainment, and even news content. Rather than informing public debate, the media have been accused of limiting such debate by reflecting the profit interests of the corporate world while minimizing the health needs of populations. In this case, the media are seen not as willing allies but as a barrier to be overcome.

Both these views represent legitimate perspectives on mass media, and they influence the emphasis that public health professionals believe should be appropriately accorded to various mass media strategies. If the media are seen as an anti-health education force, then interventions are designed to alter the nature of the health information being provided by the media. The importance of fundamental social and political factors in health promotion, often ignored by the media, is emphasized.

147

Collective rather than individual change strategies are encouraged. The media are defined as part of the problem and become not so much a mechanism for intervening as a target of intervention.

On the other hand, if the media are seen as vehicles for health promotion, then negative aspects will be viewed as relatively unimportant or even irrelevant. The key issue is packaging and distributing accurate risk factor information so that large numbers of people can presumably change their life-styles. The target of intervention is the individual, and citizens are encouraged to change their behavior to be healthier and live longer.

At a more basic level, the debate about the role of the mass media in health promotion reflects a fundamental difference about whether the pursuit of health promotion is personal-individual or social-political. If it is personal-individual, it will primarily involve being more innovative in stimulating individual behavior change. Future use of the media will be based on continued refinement and fine tuning of previous efforts to get the best information out to the most people in an appealing package. If health promotion is social-political, the role of mass media is quite different. A social-political perspective links health promotion to social change and public policy development. The focus will be on using media to address the conditions of disease rather than disease conditions. Because the mass media generally serve to reinforce existing arrangements and not stimulate social change, this perspective on health promotion represents a challenge to public health professionals and the mass media to rethink basic assumptions.

The increasing activism of public health professionals on topics such as AIDS, tobacco, nutrition and alcohol is contributing to a reexamination of the most effective strategies for using mass media. Building on lessons from several generations of public health, it has become increasingly clear that more creative, aggressive approaches are required. The purpose of this chapter is to explore the role of media as possible "disease promoters" and to present two general strategies for using mass media as an approach to health promotion.

THE MESSAGE IN THE MEDIA

Information from public health authorities designed to inform populations about health matters, no matter how extensive, is likely to account for only a small proportion of health-related content in the mass media. People are exposed to a constant stream of information about health through talk shows, news, advertising, entertainment programming, and numerous other formats in the print and electronic media. This information serves as a backdrop against which public health messages are seen or heard, thought about, understood, and, presumably, acted on by individuals. Before considering possible strategies for using mass media as an agent of health promotion, it is important to review the nature of the everyday messages about health that are communicated through the mass media.

In general, the mass media communicate several kinds of health-related content. First, specific role models are presented in that the characters in the media exhibit a range of behaviors that are relevant to health. Second, a specific perspective about the nature of health and illness is conveyed through the mass media. This perspective may condition the audience to accept particular views of disease causality and related views of health promotion. Third, consumers learn about health both directly and indirectly as a consequence of advertising. Advertising conveys strong messages about health-related products and life-styles, and it may also influence the information that news and entertainment media provide about health and well being.

Television deserves special attention because it is a primary source of health information for millions of people. For example, a recent national survey in the United States reported that television was the most frequently mentioned source of AIDS information—cited more than twice as often as newspapers and 25 times as often as physicians.

ROLE MODELS

Television is a major source of role models for a range of health-related behaviors. An extensive body of theory and research clearly indicates that there is a great potential for people to imitate televised behaviors if these behaviors are easy to execute, performed by attractive models, and generate either positive reinforcement or are reacted to in a neutral way. For example, the type of alcohol use that is commonly seen on television has the potential to promote drinking behavior in the audience. Hence, the types of health-related behavior that characters exhibit on television becomes very important from a public health perspective.

Role models on television, unfortunately, do not provide particularly useful messages regarding health. While there are notable exceptions, frequent alcohol consumption, unprotected sex, poor dietary habits and violence-centered approaches to problem solving are common themes (Gerbner, Morgan, & Signorielli, 1982). Daytime serials have been accused of conducting "a national sex disinformation campaign" (Lowry & Towles, 1989) and evening programming reflects rates of drinking far exceeding those of the real world (Wallack, Breed, & Cruz, 1987). Generally, the message of television is a glorification of instant gratification through consumption. This is reinforced in programming as well as in advertising.

CONCEPTS OF HEALTH

The way that people understand health issues is important in gaining support for health promotion efforts. If people believe health to be primarily a personal rather than a social issue, then support for *public policy* oriented approaches will likely be limited, while approaches reinforcing the responsibility of the individual will be favored. The choice here is politically important because health as a personal issue assigns responsibility to individuals while the policy oriented approach sees responsibility shared more equitably by government, the corporate world, and the individual.

Television cultivates an understanding of health that systematically reinforces the individual nature of disease and ignores or minimizes the social, economic, and political factors that are major determinants of health. Television presents a medical, rather than social, understanding of health. The medical profession is portrayed with a great deal of power and authority in the health area. Primary methods for treating illness and disease tend to be machines and drugs, with a heavy biomedical emphasis apparent. Medical care, and the disease it treats, are portrayed as apolitical and independent of larger political, economic, and social issues that are central to contemporary debates about the role of medicine in the health care system (Turow & Coe, 1985). This reinforces the concept that health and disease are ultimately matters best understood at the individual level. If the person gets sick, it is a function of life-style or the "randomness" of disease. The path to recovery is through drugs and machines—attention is to the individual but not the environment in which the individual lives.

This line of reasoning runs directly counter to what is known about the limited role of medicine in improving health status of populations. Increasing health care expenditures appear to have a limited effect on morbidity and mortality in western countries. The central message of television, according to Turow (1989), is that health care is an unlimited resource that is our primary weapon against disease.

Television also helps to shape population views of health and disease through specific dramatic movies that explore a particular disease. These "disease-of-the-week" movies cover a range of topics, including AIDS, alcoholism, breast cancer, and drugs. The movies are well intentioned and often stimulate public discussion and help reduce the stigma associated with some of these diseases. This certainly serves a useful purpose in that people may better understand some personal and technical aspects of disease (but not necessarily health) and be more tolerant of those with the problem.

Yet these movies also reinforce a fundamentally conservative view of health and the society in which it exists. The standard formula for these programs is well set. A health problem with some social stigma visits an intact, middle-class family. The family either denies the problem by making believe it does not exist or tries to deal with it by relying on internal resources. Either way, the problem creates tension in the family and strains the capacity of family members. After a period of struggle, a crisis arises, usually as a consequence of an adverse interaction with the police, friends, or a social welfare agency. The family is finally forced to seek help after it reluctantly realizes that the problem is simply too big to be handled without expert help. Help often consists of professional counseling or medical intervention. Some positive resolution is almost always reached—at the very least, hope is restored and the family unit is left intact. In the case of fatal diseases, acceptance and family unity are the positive outcome.

In these movies, the health problem is presented as a property of the individual with significant effects on the family. The causes and cures are at the family level—reinforcing the central role of the family and at the same time minimizing the importance of factors external to the family (Taylor, 1987). Collective action, political activity, or social change are seldom strategies for recovery. Social issues end up being defined as primarily individual problems. The overall effect of this type of presentation is to lessen rather than raise concern, and to provide reassurance that the problems only represent minor flaws in the system and not tears in the social fabric.

ADVERTISING

Advertising messages have been criticized as being detrimental to health in two distinct ways. First, advertising promotes the consumption of products known to be detrimental to public health. Second, the enormous economic power of the producers and advertisers may limit the presentation of accurate health information in the media.

Advertising promotes consumption to the exclusion of other values, at any cost. Alcohol and tobacco are prime examples of products that contribute significantly to excess morbidity and mortality yet are widely marketed with no regard for the damage associated with the product. Over the course of one year in the United States, the average child will see more than 22,000 television commercials—finely crafted messages dramatically presenting consumption per se as a problem-solving mechanism. Over the course of that year, it is estimated that children will see 11,000 ads for low-nutrition junk food, and adolescents will view more than 1,000 beer commercials. Advertisers promote potentially dangerous products by associating these products with peer acceptance, sexual attractiveness, success, increased self-esteem, and even, implicitly, good health. The appeals of these commercials will also systematically ignore or minimize health concerns.

The promotion of health compromising, and in some cases deadly, products through attractive life-style appeals represents a significant anti-health education force. On a broader social level, advertising does more than sell a specific product: it promotes a way of life. It is advertising as a life-style promoter, a life-style linked to a number of acute and chronic public health problems, that is of concern to public health professionals.

Advertisers easily accept the idea of disease as an individual short-coming or flaw. For example, over-the-counter advertisements treat the problems of stress, anxiety, and alienation as strictly personal and promise symptomatic relief through their products. Alcoholic beverage manufacturers blame the individual for alcohol problems, thus absolving themselves of responsibility.

This reinforces the view that the problem is personal and not social. The ultimate responsibility for problems arising from the product or from the inequalities of social organization is vested in the individual.

This individual perspective makes it acceptable to advertise the product in almost any way, and even allows advertisers to turn their skills to helping some of those who "abuse" (overeat, overdrink, drive too fast) the product through the development of public service announcements. It is not unusual to see a major brewing company urge moderation in "small letters" while promoting alcohol consumption in "giant letters." Programming, news, and advertising are partners in a general process that minimizes the role of the product, the marketplace, and the general society in the development and maintenance of preventable health problems.

In addition to the direct disinformation activities of advertising, advertising colors the way entertainment and news programming convey information and ideas. A notable case is cigarette smoking, the single most preventable cause of death in the United States. There is certainly a great need for greater awareness of the hazards of smoking and increased understanding of the complex issues involved in smoking policy. Yet a majority of school children in the United States does not believe that cigarettes should be called a drug, and vast numbers of Americans are unaware of the contribution of cigarette smoking to a wide range of chronic health problems such as heart disease (Warner, 1986).

One of the main reasons for the relatively low level of awareness of the health consequences of smoking is the more than $2 billion annually spent promoting cigarettes in the most positive light possible. But perhaps the most important reason is that Americans are denied the full story about cigarettes through mass media. A number of research studies over the past decade have repeatedly shown that editors engage in self-censorship because they are fearful of offending their tobacco advertisers.

A recent issue of *Redbook*, a popular women's magazine, provides a remarkable example of this. In an article on reducing cancer risk, a series of seven steps was recommended. Not one of these steps suggested quitting smoking, even though lung cancer is now the leading type of cancer among women.

In sum, the health message from the mass media is not a positive one. Attractive TV role models frequently exhibit behaviors providing, at best, mixed messages to the viewing audience and, at worst, instruction for an unhealthy life-style. Health issues, when presented, tend to be cast in medical terms with a primary focus on treatment, not prevention or health promotion. The political nature of public health problems is trivialized or ignored, and the social roots of health and disease are seldom presented. For the most part, health and social problems presented in the media, particularly television, tend to be defined and addressed in a noncontroversial, conservative way.

USING MASS MEDIA TO PROMOTE HEALTH

The mass media represent a paradox. On the one hand, they seem to be a substantial part of the problem—a barrier that reinforces a narrow health perspective that health promotion must overcome. Yet on the other hand the mass media represent an opportunity of the greatest magnitude. Even with all the limitations of the mass media, they still represent a promising avenue for promoting opportunity to public health goals. This is true for two reasons. First, the mass media generally feel a sense of responsibility to fill a public service role, to participate in the affairs of the community as good citizens. Media executives are opinion leaders and take their responsibility as agenda setters very seriously.

Second, the public appears to have a great interest in health issues. Topics such as oat bran and heart disease, new cancer treatments, miracle drugs, and high-tech surgical procedures can attract large audiences. Focusing on health matters can work to the benefit of media outlets. Television stations, for example, can be good community citizens, provide vital health information to consumers, and attract large audiences by participating in health-oriented public service projects. The challenge for public health professionals is to refocus media interests so that the social determinants of health are given increased visibility.

One of the well-known and crucial functions of the mass media is setting the public agenda and stimulating public discussion. The media are effective in conferring status and legitimacy on issues and thereby making it acceptable and easier to discuss these issues. This can be seen in the general case of AIDS where the word "condom" had never appeared on United States television; virtually overnight it not only was on television but it was common currency in open discussions. This power to stimulate and frame discussion is extremely important.

One of the mistakes commonly made in considering media influence is an underestimation of the importance of structuring public discussion around an issue. The way a society thinks about cigarette smoking, in the long run, may be more important than getting relatively small numbers of people to quit smoking. For example, shaping the cigarette issue around tobacco industry marketing and consumer exploitation, rather than simply getting people to quit smoking, will create a more solid foundation for long-term change. It will focus attention on the structural supports for tobacco use (e.g., advertising, economic considerations through government policies), not just the individual factors.

For the most part, however, health professionals look to the media as a way of directly changing behavior. The underlying assumption is that people adopt risky behaviors because they do not fully understand the consequences of such acts—they just don't know better. If people really knew the effects of a poor diet or of unprotected sexual activity, then they would not behave in such irresponsible ways. Ignorance is the problem, and the solution is information packaged in just the right way. Unfortunately, there is very little evidence to support the role of mass media in direct behavior change. Information is necessary but not sufficient for creating meaningful change.

The remainder of this chapter will address two approaches to using mass media for health promotion. The *social marketing* framework, combining communication and social psychology theories with applied marketing techniques, represents the current state of the art in public communication campaigning; it is increasingly used by public health professionals to promote change in individual health behaviors. Public health *media advocacy* is a relatively new approach that represents a fundamentally different "attitude" toward the mass media. It tends to target policy rather than individual issues, and it participates more aggressively in the news arena rather than relying on public service and public affairs.

SOCIAL MARKETING

Social marketing has evolved as a popular approach that attempts to apply advertising and marketing principles to the "selling" of positive health behaviors. Social marketing has become a basic strategy for addressing some of the shortcomings of previous public communication campaigns. In general, social marketing provides a framework in which marketing concepts are integrated with social-influence theories to develop programs better able to accomplish behavior change goals. It borrows the planning variables from marketing—product, price, promotion, place—and reinterprets these for a particular health issue.

The use of social marketing has been given high visibility though the careful application by community heart disease prevention programs in the United States (Farquhar, Maccoby, & Solomon, 1984) and Finland (Puska, McAlister, & Maccoby, 1985). Also, social marketers have claimed success in promoting contraceptive use and oral rehydration therapy in developing countries (Aufderheide, 1985). The positive health effects of these efforts, however, are yet to be convincingly demonstrated.

In social marketing the intervention is developed from a solid base of communication and social-psychological theories; marketing techniques are used to supplement message development and program implementation. Ideally, social marketing also involves the mobilization of local organizations and interpersonal networks as vital forces in the behavior change process. A key principle of social marketing is the reduction of psychological, social, economic, and practical distance between the consumer and the behavior.

Social marketing attempts to make it as easy and attractive as possible for the consumer to act in compliance with the message by creating the ideal marketing mix of right product, price, promotion, and place. The product is the behavior or idea that the consumer needs to accept. In some cases it is a tangible product such as a condom, and in other cases it is a behavior such as sober driving. Price can refer to psychological, social, economic, or convenience costs associated with message compliance. For example, the act of not drinking in a group can have psychological costs of anxiety and social costs of loss of status. Promotion represents how the behavior is packaged to compensate for the costs—what are the benefits, and what is the best way to communicate this message. This could include health, increased status, self-esteem, or freedom from hassle. Finally, place refers to the availability of the product or behavior. If the intervention is promoting condom use, then it is essential that condoms are widely available. Equally important to physical availability, however, is the social availability. Condoms will be more likely to be used when such use is supported and reinforced by peer groups and the community at large.

Careful definition of the problem and clear objective setting are important aspects of social marketing approaches. However, the most significant contribution of social marketing has been the strong focus on consumer needs. Consumer orientation (Lefebvre & Flora, 1988) means identifying and responding to the needs of the target audience. This is a departure from most past campaigns (and many current ones), where message and strategy development were centralized with little input from those whom the message was designed to reach.

Formative research is the primary tool for tailoring public communication efforts to specific audiences. This can be applied at all stages of intervention design and implementation and provides important feedback to the planning team. For example, small groups representing the target audience might be convened to solicit their ideas about program strategy and test their reaction to specific messages. Modifications to strategy and content can be made based on the results of these "focus" groups.

Other kinds of formative research might include analysis of the audience, so the population can be segmented into homogeneous groups; measurement of media habits of the target population, so the messages can be placed in the proper media at the proper time; and assessment of preexisting knowledge and attitudes in the target population. Formative research, when done correctly, serves to reduce some of the uncertainty associated with campaigns. Testing out possible campaign slogans, for example, can insure that such slogans are culturally sensitive and likely to be interpreted in a way that is consistent with campaign goals.

Special attention to the process of exchange is critical to the efficacy of social marketing approaches. The basis of exchange is that people are willing to exchange some resource (e.g., time, money) for a benefit (product or positive attribute). The marketing process basically attempts to facilitate a voluntary exchange that provides the consumer with tangible benefits at a minimal cost of money, physical or emotional effort, or group support. If the intervention ultimately fails to successfully facilitate this voluntary exchange, then the likelihood of effectiveness will be slight.

Social marketing has a number of limitations that inhibit its usefulness. It is an approach that has been criticized as being manipulative and ethically suspect. This is not surprising given the close correspondence to more general advertising and marketing practices.

Social marketing has also been criticized for promoting single solutions to complex health problems and ignoring the conditions that give rise to and sustain disease. For example, in developing countries social marketing will focus on changing individual health habits rather than environmental issues such as insuring a clean water supply (Aufderheide, 1985). The relatively narrow, reductionist approach of social marketing tends to reduce serious health problems to individual risk factors and ignore the proven importance of the social and economic environment as major determinants of health. In the long run this risk factor approach that forms the basis for social marketing may contribute relatively little to reducing the incidence of disease in a population.

Social marketing also faces the difficult task of motivating the voluntary exchange process with the consumer that is so crucial to its effectiveness. The limited success of typical health promotion programs which offer increased health status, positive image, and presumed peer approval in exchange for delayed gratification (e.g., diet, smoking cessation), increased physical effort (e.g., exercise), risk of social rejection (e.g., abstinence from drugs), or physical discomfort (e.g., withdrawal from cigarettes), does not provide much basis for optimism.

MEDIA ADVOCACY

"Media advocacy," according to Michael Pertschuk, one of the architects of this approach, "is the strategic use of mass media for advancing a social or public policy initiative" (*Smoking Control*, 1988). Media advocacy promotes a range of strategies to stimulate broad-based media coverage in order to reframe public debate to increase public support for more effective policy level approaches to public health problems. It does not directly attempt to change individual risk behavior but focuses attention on changing the way the problem is understood as a public health issue. For example, a media advocacy approach might develop a strategy to stimulate media coverage regarding the ethical and legal culpability of alcohol companies that promote deadly products to teenagers. The purpose is to shift attention from defining alcohol problems as solely the property of individuals, and to highlight the role of those who shape the environment in which individual decisions about health-related behavior are made.

Media advocacy is a relatively new concept that has been most closely associated with the smoking control movement in England, Australia, Canada, and the United States. Also, consumer groups concerned with alcohol, nutrition, and AIDS issues have contributed to the growing number of cases from which the principles of media advocacy are beginning to emerge.

All media coverage of health—whether news, entertainment, or public service—will tend to increase awareness and knowledge regarding health issues. Social marketing, social advertising (e.g., Partnership for a Drug Free America), and public communication campaigns in general serve this purpose. The essence of media advocacy, however, is to move beyond this function and involve the public in the policy generating process (*Smoke Signals*, 1987). For example, media advocacy in the area of nutrition would carefully use media to reframe the problem of diet from one of poor individual eating habits (an awareness and knowledge problem) to one of public policy (regulation of saturated fat in food, promotion of clear nutrition labeling). The goal is to empower the public to participate more fully in defining the social and political environment in which decisions affecting health are made.

Media advocacy is issue oriented. It recognizes that the mass media are often the forum for contesting major policies that affect health. Unfortunately, the public debate tends to be narrowly defined by ideological (individual-focused explanations) and practical (limited time to present complex issues) considerations of media coverage, and the concerns of vested interest groups. Overcoming these barriers represents a major challenge for media advocacy. It attempts to move from the "individual-simple" to the "social/political-complex" part of the problem definition continuum.

There are a number of skills that are key for the media advocate. These include research, "creative epidemiology," issue framing, and gaining access to media outlets. Research is important in becoming a reliable and credible media advocate. The advocate must not only know the key studies, significant data, and contested issues regarding the particular topic but also the characteristics of the various media outlets. For example, the nutrition activist might regularly screen the local newspaper to identify which reporters cover relevant issues or whether the paper has taken editorial positions on related issues.

Creative epidemiology is the use of new scientific evidence and existing data to gain media attention and clearly convey the public health importance of an issue. It does not imply an improper use of data or misleading presentation of the facts. On the contrary, because creative epidemiology will stimulate media coverage and, perhaps, generate controversy, it must be scientifically sound. For example, an American Cancer Society videotape explains that, "1000 people quit smoking every day—by dying. That is equivalent to 2 fully loaded jumbo jets crashing every day, with no survivors." Creative epidemiology frames data to be interesting for the media and more understandable and meaningful to the general public.

Framing the issue to be consistent with policy goals is a complex and sophisticated endeavor. The corporate world is very skilled at using valued symbols to their advantage. For example, legitimate criticism of the marketing practices of tobacco and alcohol producers becomes an "attempt at censorship" or an "assault on the First Amendment." In the United States the corporate world provides funds for local community groups, thus buying friends and goodwill. In addition, substantial support is provided to arts and cultural events in order to purchase "innocence by association" (*Smoking Control*, 1988). The industry uses a range of strategies to capture symbols (e.g., freedom of choice, freedom of speech, and patron of the arts) in order to stake out the high moral ground and gain widespread support. Variations of these themes can be seen in developing countries. In the process health educators are painted, directly or implicitly, with a host of negative images.

Successful framing of an issue puts the media advocate in a more advantageous position. The advocate can determine, to a great extent, the terms of discussion. The tobacco industry has carefully crafted an image of itself as an advocate of civil rights, protector of free speech and good community citizen. Antismoking groups were successfully characterized as zealots, health nuts, and health fascists. The industry was very successful at this until recently, when anti-smoking activists reframed the issues by stripping the industry of its positive symbols. Tobacco producers became "merchants of death," "hitmen in three-piece suits," and exploiters of youth, women, and minority groups. A number of strategies were developed to expose and publicize tobacco industry ties to cultural events, shaming through public exposure those who accept industry money, and continually making explicit the link between death and tobacco.

Successful reframing uses two primary strategies. First, it focuses attention on industry practices rather than individual behavior as a primary problem. This results in increased support for regulatory measures that can have substantial public health impact. Second, successful reframing seeks to delegitimize the industry by exposing industry practices that are exploitive and unethical. Advertising and marketing practices that exploit children and place profits before health and safety provide raw material for the media advocate. This further erodes public support for the particular industry and makes it more difficult for the industry to purchase goodwill.

Increasing access to the mass media is fundamental to media advocacy. Historically, health educators have been heavily dependent on the willingness of the media to provide time or space. In a sense, the media were allowed to define which issues would be aired and how the discussion would be structured. The availability of public service time is declining as media outlets increase efforts to sell all available slots. Even public service time now figures into bottom-line calculations (Brown, 1987). Using creative epidemiology and framing strategies, it is possible to have greater control over how the media cover an issue. To be effective it is necessary to take advantage of both free and carefully placed paid media.

It is useful to rethink the concepts of free and paid media. This usually is interpreted to mean the difference between a public service announcement, which might air at any time of the day or night, and a purchased spot that can assure the desired audience exposure to the spot. In reality there is a wide assortment of good free time for the media advocate to use.

The media advocate can create news in a number of ways. It is possible to build on breaking news stories. For example, by creating "local reaction," many communities mobilized media coverage around the release of the Surgeon General's 25th anniversary report on smoking and health. The media advocate can also create news by presenting small research studies of local or national interest. For example, the Center for Science in the Public Interest (a consumer advocacy group) drew attention to the issue of alcohol advertising and children by doing a survey that showed that children could name more brands of beer than presidents of the United States. This received national attention.

The media advocate can also build on related news opportunities. For example, when tons of Chilean fruit were banned because of a small amount of cyanide, local anti-smoking activists used this to point out to the media that it would take bushels of grapes to equal the cyanide in the sidestream smoke of just one cigarette.

There are numerous ways in which the media advocate can increase coverage of an issue. News coverage can be extended by providing op-ed pieces to newspapers and stimulating letters-to-the-editor. In addition, relationships with print and electronic journalists can be cultivated so that access is gained for follow-up stories with local perspectives. Cultivating access must be viewed as a long-term, cumulative strategy that will improve with every successful effort.

Media advocacy has several limitations. First, this approach has not been adequately defined, and no clear set of principles has been developed. It is an evolving approach that has emerged from grassroots and public interest groups. Second, the skills involved in media advocacy are probably more subtle and complex than those of the social marketer.

The media advocate needs to understand the media culture, including what is news, and how it can be framed to gain media interest and citizen support. Third, the necessary time for research and cultivating media gatekeepers may be beyond the bounds of those working in public agencies. Fourth, media advocacy is linked to an environmental approach that focuses primarily on the social and political aspects of health and is less concerned with direct behavior change. This focus makes it difficult to get and hold media attention, which tends to highlight the personal and individual aspects of health problems. Finally, media advocacy approaches will tend to be controversial because they directly confront powerful vested interests. Health agencies, as well as the media, may be hesitant to work with some advocates on some issues.

DISCUSSION

Social marketing suggests that power over health status evolves from gaining greater control over individual health behaviors. It provides people with accurate information so they can better participate in improving their own health. Media advocacy suggests that improved health status evolves from gaining greater control over the social and political environment in which decisions are made that affect health. It provides people with skills and information to better participate in changing the environment that forms the context for individual health decisions. Both approaches, if used in proper balance, have an important role to play in making the mass media more responsive to health issues.

Social marketing is a seductive concept. It serves as common ground for media outlets, community groups, government agencies, and advertisers to work together. Unfortunately, the condition for this cooperation is too often the avoidance of controversial issues and the definition of health in narrow, disease-oriented terms. It tends to be noncontroversial because it focuses on individual behaviors as the cause of disease (and presumably the cause of health) and deflects attention from products and the environment through which these products are made available. Social marketing campaigns may well contribute new opportunities for those motivated to change their health habits. On the other hand, social marketing may do little for those most in need of change but having the fewest social, economic, and personal resources to facilitate the change.

Media advocacy tries to change the rules for working with the media. It moves the focus from the public affairs section to the news departments and tries to gain greater control over the way that health issues are communicated. Media advocacy attempts to focus attention on the behavior of those whose decisions largely determine the environment (e.g., corporations, government regulators, politicians), which in turn defines the range of health choices that are available to the consumer.

Media advocacy reflects a progressive approach to health promotion in that it explicitly recognizes the importance of the environment and defines health problems as matters of public policy and not just individual behavior. Media advocacy tries to empower individuals by providing knowledge and skills to better enable them to participate in efforts to change the social and political factors that contribute to the health status of all, not just individual health behavior. The health of the community is the primary focus. Active participation in the political process becomes a mechanism for health promotion.

Social and health programs typically attempt to give people skills for beating the odds that represent the barriers to successful and healthy lives (Schorr, 1988). In the long run it makes more sense to change the odds so that more people have a wider and easier range of healthy choices to make. Social marketing is useful for developing the most creative ways to get information to people so they can beat the odds. Media advocacy helps to emphasize the importance of changing social conditions to improve the odds. This will help those most in need but often least able to change. Blending both approaches together is a start on the road to a more comprehensive approach to using the mass media to promote health. In this blending, media advocacy should be primary in order to concentrate on developing a greater understanding of the conditions for health and escape a limited focus on disease conditions.

Afterword: New Perspectives on
Health Communication

In this closing section, commentaries about emerging trends and issues involving mass media and public health are contributed by specialists representing government, media industry, advocacy, and academic perspectives. Elaine Bratic Arkin, Robert Denniston, and Rose Mary Romano appraise health communication barriers and opportunities from the federal government vantage point. Former CBS Vice President George Dessart assesses the forces reshaping the broadcasting business and the implications of the new media environment. Michael Pertschuk, who heads the Washington-based Advocacy Institute, discusses strategies for using the news media to advance public health causes. Researchers Everett Rogers and Arvind Singhal describe principles for combining entertainment with education, an increasingly influential approach for promoting public health in developing countries.

The Government Perspective

ELAINE BRATIC ARKIN
ROBERT DENNISTON
ROSE MARY ROMANO

The 1990s will witness a number of changes in the relationship between the public health community and the media. Continuing high levels of public concern about AIDS and drug abuse mean that communicating with the public about these issues remains a priority, sometimes at the expense of other health issues. Increased funding for government agencies to deal with these two national crises has produced more sophisticated media strategies, but public and policymaker expectations for success are also high; a failure to meet these sometimes unrealistic expectations could well threaten future plans to communicate through the mass media. If the AIDS and drug abuse campaigns are successful, these models could fundamentally change the standards of practice for communicating about health.

A decade of federal deregulation of the media and advertising industries has produced a ground swell of critical public reaction as the adverse results of laissez-faire policies have become apparent. For example, a growth in grass-roots advocacy activities is producing pressures for increased regulation of tobacco and alcohol advertising. In fact, the alcohol industry could soon face the kinds of controls imposed on tobacco in the 1970s. Approaches to addressing public health risks have broadened from a focus on the individual to include environmental approaches as well.

The changing needs of the public and media professionals will require changes in the way that government fulfills its responsibility to communicate health information. This commentary will examine a number of barriers to change within the government, and explore new opportunities and challenges.

Barriers to Change

Except for a few noted health problems, government budgets for health promotion and communication will probably remain stagnant. In times of fiscal belt tightening, government policymakers tend to support other priorities over communicating with the public, including media campaigns. Public affairs budgets are often an early target of budget reduction, especially if there is little evidence showing the cost effectiveness of prevention efforts when agencies focus on morbidity and mortality data.

Political interests are an important factor in deciding which programs are funded. Elected officials may perceive that community grants are more desirable than media programs, which can be seen as self-serving. Political interests can intervene in other ways as well, such as when an official becomes personally involved in a health issue or receives "bad press" from the media. As a result, carefully conceived and planned media campaigns can be waylaid by intervening political interests at virtually any time. Such interventions can occasionally produce positive results (such as the withdrawal of plans to test-market new cigarette brands as a result of Health and Human Services Secretary Sullivan's condemnation of target marketing), but these efforts can be broadly characterized as opportunistic "quick fix" solutions rather than systematic, cumulative efforts.

Many strategies outlined in these chapters require long-term commitments to change (such as developing and nurturing professional relationships with the media) or creative program management (such as developing advertising guidelines jointly with industry). Yet, most government agencies plan only one fiscal year at a time and tend to resist creativity that, by definition, stretches the rules and regulations within which government agencies operate.

These factors, along with widely varying outlooks and priorities brought about by intermittent changes in political leadership, make progress in working more closely with the media a special challenge for public health agencies. For example, federal-level "public-private sector initiatives" have been actively promoted in recent years, where once these activities were labeled a conflict of interest. Because there are few guidelines governing what constitutes a legitimate government-private enterprise effort, programs such as the Philip Morris "Bill of Rights" promotion are developed. Without explicit rules protecting the government interests in collaborative arrangements, controversial programs such as this one can disrupt other planned collaborations midstream and discourage future attempts to span the differences between government and the media industry.

Another problem is that too many health policymakers still equate media strategies solely with public service announcement (PSA) campaigns; moreover, with the declining availability of PSA slots, these policymakers cite the need for paid advertising or regulations requiring counteradvertising. As repeatedly noted in this book, there are numerous complexities involved in the relationships between the public's health and media coverage. Policymakers' lack of sophistication inhibits the development of more effective approaches and leads to other simplistic answers or a withdrawal of support altogether when PSAs do not have the desired effect (whether or not the desired effect is a realistic one).

Although experiments with paid advertising related to health issues are becoming more common, public health agencies will never be able to fund sustained nationwide campaigns at a level sufficient to compete with commercial sponsors (e.g., one brand of beer alone has a daily advertising budget of $1 million). However, there should be opportunities to include selected paid advertising (e.g., the more affordable and targeted billboard and transit spaces) in the mix of media strategies used by public health sponsors.

Organizationally, the press and public relations functions within public health agencies are separated from health education/health promotion programs targeting specific issues and special populations. This separation adds a number of constraints to media strategies, including differing priorities, budgets, expertise and outlook between staff with media responsibilities and those with health issues responsibilities.

In the public health community, few professionals are well trained to deal effectively with the media. Training programs are expensive to develop, and few opportunities exist for those who want to learn. At the same time, the media and advertising industries are in a state of economic, creative, and technological flux, challenging the public health community to keep up with changes in that sector as well as within their own sphere of responsibility.

A troublesome matter in recent years has been campaigns targeted to minorities, who are disproportionately affected by many health problems. The channels most likely to reach them (including minority media) are often those least accessible to public health agency staff, who are often more familiar with "mainstream" media. In addition, some minority media outlets may not be convinced that health issues are of interest to their audiences, may be dependent upon tobacco and/or alcohol advertisers, and may be less able to afford the donation of public service time and space.

Finally, evaluation of media programs is not always valued in government agencies and is sometimes dreaded because of lack of evaluation skills or fear of discovering and documenting failure. There is little encouragement to budget for evaluation, and there may be procedural obstacles (e.g., Office of Management and Budget clearance for federal agencies) to connecting evaluations. Policymakers are most likely to support evaluation when they are skeptical about a program, or expect to find problems; this outlook further hampers establishing a legitimate role for evaluation. As a result, there is seldom reliable documentation of the effects of media efforts sponsored by public health agencies. An often overlooked role of the government communicator is to advocate for evaluation as an inherent component of media programs.

When evaluations are performed, a number of constraints preclude most government media specialists from publishing the results of their efforts. Therefore, there is little cross-sharing of lessons learned except through word of mouth and presentations at conferences; valuable market research and other reports related to media strategies languish in government files. Agencies seldom have procedures to preserve institutional memory, and skills and experience in working with the media disappear with departing staff.

Opportunities and Outlook for the Future

Since government agencies are usually perceived as credible sources of health information, they can provide a unique service to the media and the public. Combined with the public's strong interest in media health content, there is a compelling incentive for media cooperation with public health agencies in the 1990s.

The shared interest among the media, the public, and the government in drug abuse and AIDS programs presents opportunities to stretch the traditional boundaries of how the public health and media sectors work together. New initiatives, most notably California's Proposition 99, which funds antismoking advertisements in the media, could produce new models and evidence of how health messages in the media can help improve the public's health. Other new strategies such as media advocacy (see Wallack, Chapter 11) are being explored by government agencies, but the boundaries of appropriate involvement are not yet clearly defined. There is also potential for new funding of media activities, if agencies are able to translate public concern about personal and community health into support for taxation and other legislative changes.

A major change in public health policy in the 1980s was a shift in control of programs and funding priorities from the federal level to the states. One result has been a recognition that skills are needed at all levels of government. The current strong support for "capacity building" for states and communities, including media skills, should continue well into the 1990s.

Widespread use of paid advertising by public health agencies is extremely unlikely. The costs would be extraordinary, in relation to the size of public health budgets, and there would likely be opposition by taxpayers as well as broadcasters. However, there is public and institutional (e.g., American Medical Association) support for countermessages, especially for alcohol, and for including selected media buys as one strategy within the media mix. In addition, public health agencies are producing higher quality PSAs than in the past, which stand a better chance of competing with commercial messages for the eyes and ears of the citizenry.

The Federal Trade Commission has recently stated its interest in monitoring advertising to identify misleading claims, and the Food and Drug Administration has announced draft regulations requiring labeling of food product contents. Such policy changes offer opportunities for public health agencies to highlight consumer education and to work with regulators at the state as well as the federal level to assure effective change.

In reaching "at risk" audiences, improved cost effectiveness can be achieved by replacing "shotgun" media approaches with more precise targeting strategies. For example, in the *Be Smart, Don't Start* campaign aimed at preteens (Atkin, 1989), the Office for Substance Abuse Prevention negotiated prime time and Saturday morning air time with CBS, in return for a brief exclusive access to the spots. However, public health agencies need more sophisticated capabilities to work through the most appropriate media channels. In order to take advantage of new opportunities, there is a need for strong advocacy for incorporating media strategies into government programs. In addition, expanded training, outreach, cross-sharing of talents and ideas from outside the government sector are needed to ensure that the most creative and promising media strategies become a standard part of practice within the government.

The Media Industry Perspective

GEORGE DESSART

The television industry is rapidly changing, as a fundamentally new media environment is profoundly altering the systems of mass communication in this country. Until several years ago, American television basically consisted of three major outlets rotating in public importance. With the rise of cable, independent stations and satellite-distributed networks have eroded the dominant position of ABC, CBS, and NBC. During this period, the major networks became less profitable, less regulated, and eventually less accountable to the public as new corporate executives have replaced broadcast professionals who adhered to traditional tenets of media responsibility.

Popular wisdom ascribes the changes to the effects of Federal Communication Commission deregulation, yet far more is involved. FCC abandonment of antitrafficking regulations (which prevented resale of broadcasting stations for at least three years) could not have been so influential without the coincidental dismantling of the Justice Department's antitrust division. Similarly, changes in governmental attitudes toward mergers and acquisitions brought about through leveraged buyouts made the transactions possible in the first place.

Two key factors have contributed to significant changes in the organization of the television industry. First, the rapid transition from an inflationary to a deflationary economy resulted in a decline in the growth of advertising spending. This has been compounded by several trends in the advertising industry. Mergers and acquisitions have reduced the number of national advertisers. Further, in a relaxed antitrust climate, many competing brands have disappeared. Other companies have gained such a dominance of market share as to make advertising seem less necessary. All this comes at a time when rising advertising costs together with increased emphasis on promotion, targeting, and more sophisticated research were decreasing the length of advertising flights. As a business totally dependent on advertising, network television has been especially constrained in absorbing the rising costs of production.

Second, there was an exponential growth in competition. Independent television stations with no network affiliation became profitable enough in the mid-1970s to benefit from the acquisition of off-network programming and became attractive vehicles for national advertisers making spot buys. As a result of the equalization of UHF and VHF dial positions brought about by increased cable penetration, an exponential growth in new independent stations occurred. And cable finally reached the 50% of television homes subscription level that advertisers had long said would be the market size needed to attract their significant interest.

In addition to these factors, media properties released from regulatory constraints were clearly in play in the financial markets. Leveraged buyouts of station groups and individual outlets brought enormous pressure on them, their networks, and their competitors.

For more than 50 years, growing markets and low fixed costs had made successful stations and the network-owning companies very profitable. Now, despite increased costs, the debt service requires stations to make short-term profitability the only criterion. In a climate that has made only one network profitable at any particular time during the past 10 years, network companies have sold off profitable business assets and gone through wave after wave of "downsizing" personnel cutbacks. Most of the cuts took place in the ranks of experienced employees with institutional memory. These people were replaced by a small group of persons recruited from business outside of broadcasting.

Indeed, changes at the very top brought completely inexperienced leadership into two of the three networks. At groups and stations as well, the changes meant that new leadership is no longer steeped in a concept of public accountability. A former corporate executive vice president from one of the three network-owning companies decried what he saw to be the demise of the public interest standard. "When we entered the business," he said, "we thought of ourselves as entering a priesthood!" The man who was brought in from a commercial bank to hold essentially the same job stated, "This company under this management does not recognize any such thing as a moral obligation."

Many media practitioners describe themselves as having been forced to the recognition that broadcasting companies are simply fungible assets that might better be reduced to cash if they cease to perform at a desired level of profitability.

From the perspective of the broadcaster, these changes have had profound effects on the four areas that most directly effect the communication of health information: entertainment programming, news, paid advertising, and public service announcements, and the climate of receptivity toward and awareness of health issues by the managers and professionals who staff the industry.

With only 60% of their previous level of dominance of prime-time viewing, network standards can no longer provide the leadership of the industry. Even within network programming, constraints have been relaxed. To the extent that television entertainment scripts and performances serve as exemplars in such questions as reflecting societal attitudes toward alcohol consumption, smoking, nutrition, or automobile safety, for example, society cannot look to the networks to provide the lead or to negotiate with producers toward responsibility over sensationalism. This becomes increasingly important as the lines between fact and fiction become more and more blurred.

Similarly, the national news organizations no longer occupy the leadership and standard-setting role. Increasingly, local station access to satellite-delivered coverage of news events around the world has reduced the importance of the national media as fact gatherers and fact checkers. Market driven and catering to popular taste rather than the need-to-know concept, local news operations place far less importance on such criteria as significance, comprehensiveness, and context. Both on the local and network level, budgetary constraints have dictated generalist reporters replacing trained and experienced specialists.

With short-term popularity the primary criterion, the phenomena of trash news, exploitative talk shows, confrontation for its own sake, and the celebration of the bizarre have increasingly held sway over local television.

Advertising, which has the capacity greatly to influence consumer choices affecting a number of health issues, is a special area of concern under the new corporate leadership and the highly competitive media environment. There has been a relaxation of network standards and a reduction in personnel to handle the approximately 50,000 commercials submitted each year (see Silverglade, Chapter 7).

In the area of public service announcements, the situation is one of enormous change. Although the networks continue to schedule many announcements (CBS scheduled 25,000 in 1988), local stations typically "cover" PSAs with commercial or promotion material. Indeed, surveys in some markets find a virtual disappearance of PSAs from early morning to late night. In an ominous development, some stations have instituted a policy of seeking partial payment from organizations previously given public service time.

In network prime time, ABC regularly schedules antisubstance abuse spots several times per week, CBS presents one 10-second announcement per night, and NBC has no regular prime-time PSAs although it continues to maintain its visible nightly slot in the *Tonight Show*. A major reason for fewer openings is the sharp increase in program promotions in the heightened competitive atmosphere.

Public health information providers need to consider their media relations programs in this very different environment. Many of the government and nonprofit agencies' contacts at the station and network level have left the scene, and those remaining may have suffered a decline in influence. While working toward change in the regulatory climate, the public health community would do well to develop a carefully planned campaign to contact, educate, and recruit the new media management at all levels. No other single activity will reap greater rewards in encouraging media responsibility.

The Advocacy Perspective

MICHAEL PERTSCHUK

There are at least three competing visions of the media potential and responsibility afoot in this volume, each one drawing upon a true theme from American media traditions:

The health educators evoke a vision of media as public trust, dedicated to the education of America. That vision was perhaps most lovingly embodied in the words of President Herbert Hoover as he contemplated the public education potential of the new medium of radio in 1928. "It is inconceivable that we should allow so great a possibility for service to be drowned in advertising clutter." Alas, Hoover proved more visionary than prophetic.

By contrast, the journalists also evoke a vision of public trust, but, as in Woody Allen's immortal story, in which he tells of a mythical beast with the head of a lion and the body of a lion—except that it was a different lion—journalists view their public mission not as educating, but as truth telling.

Then there are the new, unwashed: the media advocates, simultaneously idealistic and pragmatic. They rail against the excesses of the marketplace—cigarette and alcohol marketing excesses, for example—

yet their vision of the media accepts the reality of the media as market-place—responding not to duty but to alluring and exciting the readers and viewers, building and sustaining profitability.

These competing visions naturally lead to alternative strategies for approaching the media. The health educators approach, not quite hat in hand, seeking assistance from the media gatekeepers—or the advertisers who have keys to the media gates—for partnerships in health education. That can work, sometimes. It can work when the gatekeepers are in a socially responsible mood, when advertisers see benefits in the goodwill associated with being on the side of angels. It can sometimes work when the health message coincides with the commercial interests of advertisers—as when cereal companies decide to market whole grain, rather than colored sugar puffs or nutrition-drained processed flour.

But the gates swing shut as the messages challenge the very products advertised, or even the accustomed world view of the media owners. Here is where the educators come up hard against A.J. Liebling's famous gloss on the first amendment: Freedom of the press in this country, he noted, is truly available only to those who own one.

The journalists themselves say to the educators: Don't expect us to be your willing servants. We're here to report the news as we see it. If you've got news, we'll be there. If you want to make certain your messages are driven home by repetition, forget it. The first time it may be news, the second time, it's propaganda. Some, not all, may also say, "I don't get much reward for making my owner's advertisers look bad, so if you want me to write a story that makes advertisers look bad, make sure you've got a very good story."

What about Hoover's vision—the public service obligation, especially of the broadcast media, licensed to use the public airways in the public interest? Disappeared down the FCC's deregulatory rathole! A broadcast license is no more imbued today with an obligation to serve without profit, than a license to sell fish—and you don't even lose your broadcast license when you peddle rotten entertainment.

Ah, but this comes as no surprise to the media advocate. She doesn't expect much from the media. She knows it's a hard world out there in medialand. Those fortunes that have changed hands in the transfer of broadcast licenses must be recovered. If it doesn't contribute to the bottom line, then, while it may be news to the journalist it may not be suitable for the stockholder's representatives who tend the media gates.

But the health advocate knows that she possesses a news key to the heart of the journalist, and the commercial key to the heart of the media entrepreneur. Van Gordon Sauter gives us the secret: health news sells. Health and wellness are by far the most popular discretionary news subject, he tells us. At least one out of every four articles in daily newspapers is health related. It's a winner for building and sustaining viewership and readership.

So the media advocate approaches the gatekeepers not as supplicant but as the vendor of a valued commodity. That's the good news. But the challenge to the media advocate is to deliver good stories. Not all health stories are newsworthy. And even good stories won't be repeated—unless, that is, they are transformed into new stories.

So the first task of the media advocate—and perhaps the first task of the health educator—is to recognize a good story and know how to market it. But the greatest art of the media advocate is to recognize a nonstory—and transform it into a story.

Mere "ink" is not the ultimate goal of the media advocate. The story may or may not serve the strategic goal of the media advocate, which is to advance a public policy goal by raising the public awareness and support. Indeed, the goal of gaining the media's attention with a good story may actually conflict with the advocate's need to frame the story as a public health issue.

So the media health educator is advised to make the story personal, show "the face of the victim." Automobile safety is rarely a story; automobile crashes are almost always a story. But most crash stories tell us nothing about the environmental causes of the crash. If the driver was drinking, we'll probably learn about it. If the driver was a teenager, we'll probably be told. But we will most likely not be reminded that the teenager's drinking was stimulated and reinforced by a media environment abloom with billboard ads and clangorous ballgame commercials and sponsored spring beer busts.

So the media advocate needs to know almost as much about who makes a news story as the journalist. She needs to know almost as much as the journalist in order to shape the material of the story she wants to tell into a marketable story. And she needs to know what the journalist does not care to know: how to frame the story so as to advance public policy goals.

There is the subterranean clash of professional cultures hovering about this book—not to neglect hints of populism versus free market individualism; the media craft lore of the advocate versus the academic rigor (and, perhaps, rigidity) of the social psychologist; the commitment of the advocate versus the passion for detachment of the journalist.

There was a certain amount of posturing in this conference, especially from the media participants who trumpeted their dedication to their noble first amendment role but did not care to speak of their devotion to making money. Ironically, many of the best journalists, who insist they are not advocates for health, do not do themselves full justice (or injustice). For we all have known journalists who care deeply about the overreaching greed of the tobacco and alcohol pushers, and who are silent (and sometimes not-so-silent) allies in the framing of stories that evoke appropriate outrage at these companies and their marketing excesses.

With all competing notes and tunes, there is yet one common theme that threads its way through the domains of the journalists, the educators, and the advocates: know thy media as thy would thy nose! Know what makes it tick, and it will tick for thee. If you possess the soul of St. Francis and the media savvy of a *60 Minutes* producer, you may save more lives at about the same cost as St. Francis himself.

The Academic Perspective

EVERETT M. ROGERS
ARVIND SINGHAL

Researchers have recently examined a promising approach to health promotion that emphasizes an entertaining style of presentation. The entertainment-education strategy amounts to intentionally inserting educational content in entertainment messages, whether in radio, television, print, or popular music. This strategy thus combines two forms of mass media—entertainment and information campaigns—that are treated mainly in a discrete fashion in previous chapters of the present book. Our present review of uses of the entertainment-education strategy centers mainly on the Third World nations of Latin America, Africa, and Asia, where this strategy has been utilized exclusively in development programs in recent years. We shall draw a series of general lessons from these experiences, concentrating on health-related campaigns.

Combining Entertainment with Education

A time-honored and seldom-questioned classification of media messages is whether they are educational or entertaining in nature. There is not complete agreement on what to call the entertainment-education communication strategy that has been utilized in recent years. Various alternatives, such as "pro-development," "enter-education," and "edutainment" have been proposed (Rogers, Aikat, Chang, Poppe, & Sopory, 1989). Everyone agrees, however, that the key idea is to combine entertainment and education so as to obtain certain advantages of each.

Entertainment-Education via Television

The conception of entertainment-education television soap operas originated in 1974 with Televisa, the Mexican commercial television network. These soap operas were the idea of Miguel Sabido, an internationally acclaimed Mexican theater director and a writer-producer-director at Televisa. Sabido designed seven entertainment-education soap operas that were broadcast in Mexico from 1975 to 1982. *Acompáñame* ("Accompany Me") promoted family planning in Mexico during 1977-1978, achieved high audience ratings, and, along with other factors, convinced half a million Mexicans to visit government family-planning health clinics (Televisa's Institute of Communication Research, 1981). Sabido's other soap operas in Mexico dealt with female equality, child rearing, and sex education for teenagers.

The Mexican soap opera experience inspired India to broadcast *Hum Log* ("We People"), a 1984-1985 television series addressing such social issues as gender inequality, health, alcoholism, and family planning (Singhal & Rogers, 1989). Most *Hum Log* viewers reported learning positive attitudes and behaviors about an equal status for women, national integration, health, and smaller family-size norms. At the close of each episode, a famous actor in Hindi films, Ashok Kumar, briefly summarized that episode in the television series, providing viewers with appropriate guides to action. Each epilogue of approximately 30 to 50 seconds was a concentrated educational message, drawing out key lessons for behavior change.

Hum Log's audience success persuaded Kenya to broadcast its first family planning television soap opera, *Tushauriane* ("Let's Discuss"), from 1987 to 1989. In 1990, Mexico's Miguel Sabido is producing another family-planning soap opera (with an AIDS-prevention and drug-abuse subtheme) *Sangre Joven* ("Young Blood"), to be broadcast in six Latin American nations and on Spanish-language television in the United States (Singhal, 1990).

In Enugu, Nigeria, the Nigeria Television Authority (NTA), in collaboration with Johns Hopkins University's Population Communication Services (JHU/PCS), integrated family-planning themes in the drama segments of an existing television variety show, *In a Lighter Mood*. Thirty-nine episodes were broadcast for 14 months during 1986-1987. The family-planning television segments promoted the benefits of child spacing, modern methods of contraception, and small family-size norms (Winnard, Rimon, & Convisser, 1987). Twice during each episode, Enugu's only family-planning clinic was advertised, encouraging residents to seek help in family-planning matters.

Point-of-referral data were gathered at the only family-planning clinic in Enugu. A 147% increase occurred in the number of adopters of family planning over the 14 months after the broadcasts began, and 60% of all new adopters reported the television program as their source of referral to the clinic.

In Egypt, *Ana Zananna* ("I'm Persistent"), a humorous television series consisting of 14 television minidramas (each one minute long), provided education about family-planning methods to a nationwide television audience in Egypt. Broadcast over 100 times (almost like an advertising spot) in 1988, each episode of *Ana Zananna* was a self-contained melodramatic television spot. A research evaluation showed the *Ana Zananna* family-planning campaign to be very effective. In 1988, Turkish Television broadcast a similar family-planning television miniseries, *Sparrows Don't Migrate*, which was watched by about 20 million Turks.

Entertainment-Education via Radio and Music

In recent years, a number of pioneering efforts has been made in radio to break down the arbitrary dichotomy of entertainment versus education. From 1985 to 1989, Elaine Perkins wrote and produced a family-planning radio soap opera, *Naseberry Street*, for the Jamaican Family Planning Association. *Naseberry Street* reached an audience of about one million, 40% of Jamaica's population. Evaluation research showed that the radio soap opera is highly effective in promoting the adoption of family planning in Jamaica (Stone, 1988). Similar efforts utilizing an entertainment-education strategy in radio have occurred in Indonesia, Kenya, and Costa Rica.

One of the most effective means of reaching the public, especially teenagers, is to convey educational messages through popular music. From 1982 to 1986, the Jamaican National Family Planning Board ran an integrated family-planning communication campaign that included songs about sexual responsibility. One of the key slogans of this family-planning campaign was "Before you be a mother, you got to be a woman." This slogan was the chorus of a song that was sung to a catchy reggae beat by Gem Myers and the Fab Five, a popular music group in Jamaica. This song became very popular with the teenage Jamaican audience. A 1986 evaluation showed that about 90% of the respondents recalled the sexual responsibility message in "You got to be a woman" (*Population Reports*, 1986).

In 1986, Johns Hopkins University's Population Communication Services (JHU/PCS) launched a unique communication project in Spanish-speaking Latin American countries: A rock music video that promoted sexual abstinence and contraception, entitled *Cuando Estemos Juntos* ("When We Are Together"). This song was number one on the pop music charts within six weeks of its release in Mexico, and soon it was also a top-rated song in 11 other Latin American countries. Tatiana, a 16-year old singer from Mexico, and Johnny, a 17-year old Puerto Rican singer, performed *Cuando Estemos Juntos*. The teenage singers told their teenage audience not to have sex. Radio and television stations could play the song without paying a broadcast fee if they accompanied the music with an announcement of the address and telephone number of a local family-planning clinic that offered contraceptive services to teenagers (Kincaid, Jara, Coleman, & Segura, 1988).

In 1988, a similar rock music campaign was launched by JHU/PCS officials in the Philippines to promote sexual responsibility among Filipino teenagers. As in the case of Tatiana and Johnny's song in Mexico, JHU/PCS's multimedia efforts in the Philippines had two components: commercial and institutional. The commercial component attempted to establish each song as a commercial hit with a social message. The institutional component linked the song's message to a telephone hotline, where young adults received information, counseling, and referrals about their problems.

Lessons Learned About the Entertainment-Education Strategy

Here we draw a series of general lessons from the use of entertainment-education strategy in Third World countries, concentrating on health-related campaigns.

The mixture of entertainment and educational message content can serve to attract large audiences to the media and thus earn high profits from advertising and/or sales (Singhal & Rogers, 1989). Education is ordinarily a cost, and often it is a huge and expensive drain on the national exchequer. In comparison, the entertainment-education strategy provides an opportunity for an educational message to pay for itself, and often to yield a profit. For example, the popularity of *Cuando Estemos Juntos* led to record-breaking sales of Tatiana's music album.

The entertainment-education communication cannot make the educational content too blatant or hard-sell, or else the audience will reject such messages (Singhal & Rogers, 1989). How much education should be included in an entertainment-education message? No hard-and-fast rule is available, but experiences to date suggest that overemphasized educational content can turn off the intended audience.

The effects of using the entertainment-education strategy are increased when the entertainment-education strategy is accompanied by supplementary messages to form an integrated communication campaign (Rogers & Singhal, 1989). The rock songs promoting sexual responsibility among teenagers in Mexico and in the Philippines were accompanied by print and broadcast advertisements, personal appearances by the singers, label buttons urging "Say No to Sex," posters, and a telephone ("Dial-A Friend") hotline. These attempts at behavior change consisted of a coordinated communication campaign, rather than just a song featuring lyrics with an educational message.

The repetition of the educational content in an entertainment-educational message is important in achieving its desired educational effects (Rogers & Singhal, 1989). Compared to the results of most communication research on a single message (which typically finds only minimal effects), studies of the effects of entertainment-education messages show they have considerable effects. Why? One reason is repetition. A television soap opera is typically broadcast for one hour per day, five days a week, for a year or more. Similarly, a hit song like *Cuando Estemos Juntos* was played by a typical Mexican radio station about 15 times *per day* for the 3 or 4 months of the song's greatest popularity! On the other hand, a single-shot dedicated episode of prime-time program is likely to have little impact.

Entertainment-education communication strategies are most successful when public health officials, broadcast media officials, development planners, religious organizations, commercial sponsors, and other involved parties work collaboratively. Such a collaboration creates consensus between participating organizations and facilitates coordination of the public service infrastructure. For example, the success of *Acompáñame* can be attributed to the cooperation among Mexican government officials, family-planning organizations, the Catholic Church, Televisa (the Mexican national television network), and the infrastructure of government clinics (Singhal, 1990).

Also, several champions in a nation must become interested in an entertainment-education mass medium and put the weight of their position behind the idea for the idea to be carried forward into action (Rogers & Singhal, 1989). So ultimately the success of an entertainment-education project depends on committed leadership.

References

AAF hears warnings of turning tide. (1988). *Broadcasting, 114*(12), 46.

Altman, D. G., Slater, M. D., Albright, C. L., & Maccoby, N. (1987). How an unhealthy product is sold: Cigarette advertising in magazines, 1960-1985. *Journal of Communication, 37*(4), 95-106.

Atkin, C. K. (1976). Children's social learning from television advertising: Research evidence on observational modeling of product consumption. *Advances in Consumer Research, 3*, 513-519.

Atkin, C. K. (1978). Effects of drug commercials on young viewers. *Journal of Communication, 28*(2), 81-89.

Atkin, C. K. (1980). Effects of television advertising on children. In E. L. Palmer & A. Dorr (Eds.), *Children and the faces of television: Teaching, violence, and selling* (pp. 287-306). New York: Academic Press.

Atkin, C. K. (1981). Mass media information campaign effectiveness. In R. E. Rice & W. J. Paisley (Eds.), *Public communication campaigns* (pp. 265-279). Beverly Hills, CA: Sage.

Atkin, C. K. (1989). Be Smart. Don't Start! In R. E. Rice & C. K. Atkin (Eds.), *Public communication campaigns* (pp. 224-227). Newbury Park, CA: Sage.

Atkin, C. K., & Block, M. (1980). *Content and effect of alcoholic beverages advertising.* Final report prepared for the Bureau of Alcohol, Tobacco and Firearms, the Federal Trade Commission, the Department of Transportation, and NIAAA. Department of Communication, Michigan State University.

Atkin, C. K., & Freimuth, V. (1989). Formative evaluation research in campaign design. In R. E. Rice & C. K. Atkin (Eds.), *Public communication campaigns* (pp. 131-150). Newbury Park, CA: Sage.

Atkin, C. K., & Gibson, W. (1978). *Children's nutrition learning from television advertising.* Unpublished manuscript, Michigan State University.

Atkin, C. K., & Heald, G. (1977). The content of children's toy and food commercials. *Journal of Communication, 27*(1), 107-114.

Atkin, C. K., Hocking, J., & Block, M. (1984). Teenage drinking: Does advertising make a difference? *Journal of Communication, 34*(2), 157-167.

Atkin, C. K., Neuendorf, K., & McDermott, S. (1983). The role of alcohol advertising in excessive and hazardous drinking. *Journal of Drug Education, 13*(4), 313-325.

Aufderheide, P. (1985). Huckstering health. *Channels, 5*(1), 51-52.

Backer, T. (1988). Health professionals' and mass media's campaigns to prevent AIDS and drug abuse. *Counseling and Human Development, 20*(7), 1-10.

Bagdikian, B. (1983). *The media monopoly.* Boston: Beacon.

Bandura, A. (1977). *Social learning theory.* Englewood Cliffs, NJ: Prentice-Hall.

Bandura, A. (1978). Self-efficacy: Toward a unifying theory of behavioral change. *Psychological Review, 84*, 191-215.

Bandura, A. (1986). *Social foundations of thought and action: A social cognitive theory.* Englewood Cliffs, NJ: Prentice-Hall.

Barcus, F. E. (1976). Over-the-counter and proprietary drug advertising on television. In R. E. Ostman (Ed.), *Communication research and drug education* (pp. 89-111). Beverly Hills, CA: Sage.

Barcus, F. E. (1980). The nature of television advertising to children. In E. L. Palmer & A. Dorr (Eds.), *Children and faces of television: Teaching, violence, and selling* (pp.273-285). New York: Academic Press.

Barnard, C. N. (1973). Medicine and the mass media. *American Journal of Cardiology, 21*, 112-131.

Barnouw, E. (1978). *The sponsor.* New York: Oxford University Press.

Bauer, R. (1964). The obstinate audience: The influence process from the point of view of social communication. *American Psychologist, 19*, 319-328.

Bauman, K. E., Brown, J. D., Bryan, E. S., Fisher, L. A., Padgett, C. A., & Sweeney, J. M. (1989). Three mass media campaigns to prevent adolescent cigarette smoking. *Preventive Medicine, 17*(5), 510-530.

Becker, M. H. (1974). *The health belief model and personal health behavior.* Thorofare, NJ: Slack.

Beltramini, R. F. (1988). Perceived believability of warning label information presented in cigarette advertising. *Journal of Advertising, 17*(1), 26-32.

Blumler, J. G., & Katz, E. (Eds.). (1974). *The uses of mass communications.* Beverly Hills, CA: Sage.

Bolton, R. N. (1983). Modeling the impact of television food advertising on children's diets. *Current Issues and Research in Advertising, 3,* 173-199.

Breed, W. J., & De Foe, J. R. (1981). The portrayal of the drinking process on primetime television. *Journal of Communication, 31*(1), 58-67.

Breed, W. J., & De Foe, J. R. (1982). Effecting media change: The role of cooperative consultation on media topics. *Journal of Communication, 32*(2), 88-99.

Breed, W. J., & De Foe, J. R. (1984). Drinking and smoking on television, 1950-1982. *Journal of Public Health Policy, 5*(2), 257-270.

Brown, J. D., Childers, K. W., & Waszak, C. S. (1989). Television and adolescent sexuality. *Journal of Adolescent Health Care, 10,* 64-78.

Brown, J. D., & Newcomer, S. F. (in press). Influences of television and peers on adolescents' sexual behavior. *Journal of Homosexuality*.

Brown, L. (1987). Hype in a good cause. *Channels*, 7(7), 26.

Cantor, M. (1988). *The Hollywood TV producer: His work and his audience*. New York: Basic Books.

Cantor, M. (1979). The politics of popular drama. *Communication Research*, 6, 387-406.

Cantor, M. (1980). *Prime-time television: Content and control*. Beverly Hills, CA: Sage.

Cartwright, D. (1949). Some principles of mass persuasion: Selected finding of research on the sale of United States war bonds. *Human Relations*, 2, 253-267.

Choate, R. B. (1975). *Statement before the Subcommittee on Communications of the Committee on Interstate and Foreign Commerce*. Washington, DC: United States House of Representatives.

Choate, R. B. (1976). *Testimony before the Federal Trade Commission in the matter of a trade regulation rule on food nutrition advertising*. Washington, DC: Council on Children, Media and Merchandising.

Clancey-Hepburn, K., Hickey, A. A., & Neville, G. (1974). Children's behavior responses to TV food advertisements. *Journal of Nutrition Education*, 6, 93-96.

Colburn, D. (1987, February). Pursuing the disease of the moment. *Columbia Journalism Review*, 8-9.

Colman, W. (1990). *Health moves to prime time: Evaluating the impact of a prime-time television movie of the week on viewers' content-relevant health beliefs*. Unpublished doctoral dissertation, University of California, Los Angeles.

Combs, B., & Slovic, P. (1979). Newspaper coverage of causes of death. *Journalism Quaterly*, 65, 837-849.

Cook, J., & Lewington, M. (1979). *Images of alcoholism*. London: British Film Institute.

Culbertson, H. M., & Stempel, G. H. (1984). Possible barriers to agenda setting in medical news. *Newspaper Research Journal*, 5(3), 53-60.

Davis, J. L. (1987). Given the obstacles to doing effective commercials for Rx drugs, how do any get on the air at all? *Medical Advertising News*, 23, 6-7.

Dearing, J. W., & Rogers, E. M. (1988). *The agenda-setting process for the issue of AIDS*. Paper presented at the annual conference of the International Communication Association.

De Foe, J. R., Breed, W., & Wallack, L. (1983). Drinking on television: A five-year study. *Journal of Drug Education*, 13(1), 25-38.

DeJong, W., & Winsten, J. A. (in press). Recommendations for future mass media campaigns to prevent preteen and adolescent substance abuse. *Health Affairs*.

DeVries, W. C. (1988). The physician, the media, and the spectacular case. *Journal of the American Medical Association*, 886.

Dietz, W. H. (1989). You are what you eat: What you eat is what you are. *Journal of Adolescent Health Care*, 10, 41-50.

Dietz, W. H., & Gortmaker, S. L. (1985). Do we fatten our children at the TV set? Television viewing and obesity in children and adolescents. *Pediatrics*, 75, 807-812.

Donohue, T. (1975). Effect of commercials on black children. *Journal of Advertising Research*, 15(6), 41-46.

Donohue, T., Meyer, T., & Henke, L. (1978). Black and white children's perceptions of television commercials. *Journal of Marketing*, 42, 34-40.

Dunwoody, S. (1980). The science writing inner club: A communication link between science and the lay public. *Science, Technology and Human Values*, 5(3), 14-22.

Dunwoody, S., & Ryan, M. (1984). Scientific barriers to the popularization of science in the mass media. *Journal of Communication, 35*(1), 26-40.

Faber, R. J., Meyer, T. P., & Miller, M. M. (1984). The effectiveness of health disclosures within children's television commercials. *Journal of Broadcasting, 28*(4), 463-476.

Farquhar, J., Maccoby, N., & Solomon, D. (1984). Community applications of behavioral medicine. In W. Gentry (Ed.), *Handbook of behavioral medicine* (pp. 437-478). New York: Guilford Press.

Fishbein, M., & Ajzen, I. (1975). *Belief, attitude, intention and behavior: An introduction to theory and research.* Reading, MA: Addison-Wesley.

Flay, B. R. (1981). On improving the chances of mass media health promotion programs causing meaningful changes in behavior. In M. Meyer (Ed.), *Health education by television and radio* (pp. 56-89). Munich: Saur.

Flay, B. R. (1986a). Mass media linkages with school-based programs for drug abuse prevention. *Journal of School Health, 56*(9), 402-406.

Flay, B. R. (1986b). Efficacy and effectiveness trials (and other stages of research) in the development of health promotion programs. *Preventive Medicine, 15*(5), 451-474.

Flay, B. R. (1987a). Evaluation of the development, dissemination and effectiveness of mass media health programming. *Health Education Research, 2*(2), 123-130.

Flay, B. R. (1987b). Mass media and smoking cessation: A critical review. *American Journal of Public Health, 77*(2), 153-160.

Flay, B. R. (1987c). *Selling the smokeless society: 56 evaluated programs and campaigns worldwide.* Washington, DC: American Public Health Association.

Flay, B. R. (in press). Mass media and smoking cessation. In G. Comstock (Ed.), *Public communication and behavior* (vol. 3). New York: Academic Press.

Flay, B. R., & Cook, T. D. (1981). Evalution of mass media prevention campaigns. In R. E. Rice & W. J. Paisley (Eds.), *Public communication campaigns* (pp. 239-264). Beverly Hills, CA: Sage.

Flay, B. R., & Cook, T. D. (1989). Three models for evaluating prevention campaigns with a mass media component. In R. E. Rice & C. K. Atkin (Eds.), *Public communication campaigns* (pp. 175-196). Newbury Park, CA: Sage.

Flay, B. R., Brannon, B. R., Johnson, C. A., Hansen, W. B., Ulene, A., Whitney-Saltiel, D. A., Gleason, L. R., Gavin, D. M., Glowacz, K. M., Sobol, D. F., Spiegel, D.C., & Sussman, S. (1988). The television, school and family prevention/cessation project: I. Theoretical basis and television program development. *Preventive Medicine, 17*(5), 585-607.

Flay, B. R., d'Avernas, J. R., Best, J. A., Kersell, M. W., & Ryan, K. B. (1983). Cigarette smoking: Why young people do it and ways of preventing it. In P. J. McGrath & P. Firestone (Eds.), *Pediatric and adolescent behavioral medicine* (pp. 132-183). New York: Springer.

Flay, B. R., Hansen, W. B., Johnson, C. A., Collins, L. M., Dent, C. W., Dwyer, K. M., Hockstein, G., Gossman, L., Rauch, J., Sobol, D. F., Sobol, J. L., Sussman, S. Y., & Ulene, A. (1987). Implementation effectiveness trial of a social influences prevention program using schools and television. *Health Education Research, 2*(4), 385-400.

Flay, B. R., Kessler, R.C., & Utts, J. M. (1989). Evaluating media campaigns. In S. L. Coyle, R. F. Boruch, & C. F. Turner (Eds.), *Evaluating AIDS prevention programs* (pp. 312-336). Washington, DC: National Academy Press.

Freimuth, V. S., Greenberg, R. H., DeWitt, J., & Romano, R. M. (1984). Covering cancer: Newspapers and the public interest. *Journal of Communication, 34*(1), 62-73.

Freimuth, V. S., Hammond, S. L., & Stein, J. A. (1988). Health advertising: Prevention for profit. *American Journal of Public Health, 78*(5), 557-561.

Gandy, O. H. (1982). *Beyond agenda setting*. Norwood, NJ: Ablex.

Gerbner, G., & Gross, L. (1976). Living with television: The violence profile. *Journal of Communication, 26*(2), 173-179.

Gerbner, G., Gross, L., Morgan, M., & Signorielli, N. (1981). Health and medicine on television. *New England Journal of Medicine, 305*(15), 901-904.

Gerbner, G., Morgan, M., & Signorielli, N. (1982). Programming health portrayals: What viewers see, say and do. In D. Pearl, L. Bouthilet, & J. Lazar (Eds.), *Television and behavior: Ten years of scientific progress and implications for the eighties* (pp. 291-307). Rockville, MD: National Institute of Mental Health.

Gitlin, T. (1979). Prime-time ideology: The hegemonic process in television entertainment. *Social Problems, 26*, 251-266.

Gitlin, T. (1983). *Inside prime time*. New York: Pantheon.

Goldberg, M. E., & Gorn, G. (1978). Some unintended consequences of TV advertising to children. *Journal of Consumer Research, 5*(2), 22-29.

Goldberg, M. E., Gorn, G. J., & Gibson, W. (1978). TV messages for snack and breakfast foods: Do they influence children's preferences? *Journal of Consumer Research, 5*, 73-81.

Goldstein, T. (1985). *The news at any cost*. New York: Simon & Schuster.

Greenberg, B. S. (1981). Smoking, drugging and drinking in top rated TV series. *Journal of Drug Education, 11*(3), 227-233.

Greenberg, B. S., Abelman, R., & Neuendorf, K. (1981). Sex on the soap operas: An afternoon delight. *Journal of Communication, 31*(3), 83-89.

Greenberg, B. S., & Atkin, C. K. (1983). The portrayal of driving on television, 1975-1980. *Journal of Communication, 33*(2), 44-55.

Greenberg, B. S., Fernandez-Collado, C., Graef, D., Korzenny, F., & Atkin, C. K. (1979). Trends in the use of alcohol and other substances on television. *Journal of Drug Education, 9*(3), 243-253.

Greenberg, B. S., Graef, D., Fernandez-Collado, C., Korzenny, F., & Atkin, C. K. (1980). Sexual intimacy on commercial television during prime time. In B. S. Greenberg (Ed.), *Life on television: Content analyses of U.S. TV drama* (pp. 129-136). Norwood, NJ: Ablex.

Greenberg, B. S., Linsangan, R. L., Soderman, A., Dorfman, S., Heeter, C., & Stanley, C. (1987). Adolescents and their exposure to television and movie sex. Project CAST Report #4, Department of Telecommunication, Michigan State University.

Greenberg, B. S., Siemicki, M., Dorman, S., Heeter, C., Stanley, C., Soderman, A., & Linsangan, R. (1986a). *Sex content in R-rated films viewed by adolescents*. Project CAST Report #3, Department of Telecommunication, Michigan State University.

Greenberg, B. S., Stanley, C., Siemicki, M., Heeter, C., Soderman, A., & Linsangan, R. (1986b). *Sex content on soaps and primetime television series most viewed by adolescents*. Project CAST Report #2, Department of Telecommunication, Michigan State University.

Greeson, L. E., & Williams, R. A. (1986). Social implications of music videos for youth: An analysis of the content and effects of MTV. *Youth & Society, 18*(2), 177-189.

Hanneman, G. J., & McEwen, W. J. (1976). The use and abuse of drugs: An analysis of mass media content. In R. E. Ostman (Ed.), *Communication research and drug education* (pp. 65-88). Beverly Hills, CA: Sage.

Healthy people: The Surgeon General's report on health promotion and disease prevention. (1979). Washington, DC: Government Printing Office.

Heeter, C., Perlstadt, H., & Greenberg, B. S. (1984). *Health incidents, stages of illness and treatment on popular television programs.* Paper presented at the annual convention of the International Communication Association.

Kahle, L. R., Poulous, B., & Sukhdial, A. (1988). Changes in social values in the United States during the past decade. *Journal of Advertising Research, 28*(2), 35-41.

Katz, E. (1980). On conceptualizing media effects. In C. McCormack (Ed.), *Studies in communications* (vol. 1, pp. 171-192). Greenwich, CT: JAI Press.

Katz, E., & Lazarsfeld, P. R. (1955). *Personal influence.* New York: Free Press.

Kaufman, L. (1980). Prime time nutrition. *Journal of Communication, 30*(3), 37-46.

Kincaid, D. L., Jara, J. R., Coleman, P., & Segura, F. (1988). *Getting the message: The communication for young people project.* Washington, DC: U.S. Agency for International Development, AID Evaluation Study 56.

Klaidman, S., & Beauchamp, T. L. (1986, summer). Baby Jane Doe in the media. *Journal of Health, Politics, Policy and Law,* 277.

Klaidman, S., & Beauchamp, T. L. (1987). *The virtuous journalist.* New York: Oxford University Press.

Klein, T., & Danzig, F. (1985). *Publicity: How to make the media work for you.* New York: Charles Scribner's Sons.

Lazarsfeld, P. F., & Merton, R. K. (1948). Mass communication, popular taste and organized social action. In W. Schramm (Ed.), *Mass communication* (pp. 492-512). Urbana: University of Illinois Press.

Lefebvre, C., & Flora, J. (1988). Social marketing and public health intervention. *Health Education Quarterly, 15*(3), 299-315.

Levenkron, J., & Farquhar, J. (1982). Recruitment using mass media strategies. *Circulation, 66,* 32-36.

Leventhal, H., & Cleary, P. (1980). The smoking problem: A review of the research and theory in behavioral risk modification. *Psychological Bulletin, 88,* 370-405.

Levy, A., & Stokes, R. (1987). Effects of a health promotion advertising campaign on sales of ready to eat cereals. *Public Health Reports, 102*(4), 398-403.

Lichtenstein, E., & Mermelstein, R. (1984). Review of approaches to smoking treatment strategies. In J. D. Matarazzo, N. E. Miller, S. M. Weiss, & J. A. Herd (Eds.), *Behavioral health: A handbook of health enhancement and disease prevention.* New York: John Wiley.

Liebling, A. J. (1961). *The press.* New York: Ballantine.

Lowry, D., & Towles, D. (1989). Soap opera portrayals of sex, contraception and sexually transmitted diseases: A public health perspective. *Journal of Communication, 39*(2), 76-83.

Maccoby, N., & Alexander, J. (1980). Use of media in lifestyle programs. In P. Davidson & S. Davidson (Eds.), *Behavioral medicine: Changing health lifestyles* (pp. 351-370). New York: Brunner/Mazel.

Maccoby, N., & Solomon, D. S. (1981). Heart disease prevention: Community studies. In R. E. Rice & W. J. Paisley (Eds.), *Public communication campaigns* (pp. 105-126). Beverly Hills, CA: Sage.

MacDonald, P. T. (1983). The "dope" on soaps. *Journal of Drug Education, 13*(4), 359-368.

Marmot, M., Kogevinas, M., & Elston, M. (1987). Social/economic status and disease. *Annual Review of Public Health, 8,* 111-135.

McAlister, A. L., Puska, P., & Salonen, J. T. (1982). Theory and action for health promotion: Illustrations from the North Karelia Project. *American Journal of Public Health, 72*, 43-50.

McCombs, M. E., & Shaw, D. L. (1972). The agenda-setting function of the media. *Public Opinion Quarterly, 36*, 176-188.

McCron, R., & Budd, J. (1981). The role of mass media in health education: An analysis. In M. Meyer (Ed.), *Health education by television and radio* (pp. 90-102). Munich: Saur.

McEwen, W. J., & Hanneman, G. J. (1974). The depiction of drug use in television programming. *Journal of Drug Education, 4*(3), 281-293.

McGuire, W. J. (1984). Public communications as a strategy for inducing health-promoting behavior change. *Preventive Medicine, 13*(3), 299-319.

McGuire, W. J. (1985). Attitudes and attitude change. In G. Lindzey & E. Aronson (Eds.), *Handbook of social psychology* (vol. 2, 3rd ed., pp. 233-346). New York: Random House.

McKinlay, J. (1979). A case for refocussing upstream: The political economy of illness. In E. Jaco (Ed.), *Patients, physicians and illness* (pp. 71-82). New York: Free Press.

McLaughlin, J. (1975). The doctor shows. *Journal of Communication, 25*(3), 182-184.

Mechanic, D. (1982). Disease, mortality, and the promotion of health. *Health Affairs, 1*(3), 28-32.

Mendelsohn, H. (1973). Some reasons why information campaigns can succeed. *Public Opinion Quarterly, 37*, 50-61.

Meyer, P. (1987). *Ethical journalism.* New York: Longman.

Milavsky, J. R. (1988). *What media can do to alleviate the AIDS problem.* Paper presented at Communications Industry Forum, University of California, Santa Barbara.

Milavsky, J. R., Pekowsky, B., & Stipp, H. (1975-1976). TV drug advertising and proprietary and illicit drug use among teenage boys. *Public Opinion Quarterly, 39*(4), 457-481.

Minkler, M., Wallack, L., & Madden, P. (1987). Alcohol and cigarette advertising in *Ms.* magazine. *Journal of Public Health Policy, 8*(2), 164-179.

Mirotznik, J., & Mosellie, B. M. (1986). Genital herpes and the mass media. *Journal of Popular Culture, 20*, 1-11.

Montgomery, K. (1981). Gay activists and the networks: A case study of pressure. *Journal of Communication, 31*(2), 49-57.

Montgomery, K. (1989). *Target: Prime time. Advocacy groups and the struggle over entertainment television.* New York: Oxford University Press.

Morley, D. D., & Walker, K. B. (1987). The role of importance, novelty and plausability in producing belief change. *Communication Monographs, 54*, 436-442.

Murrow, E. R. (1958, November 13). A broadcaster talks to his colleagues. *The Reporter.*

Newcomb, H. (1983). *The producer's medium: Conversations with creators of American TV.* New York: Oxford University Press.

Nielsen Media Research. (1987). *1987 Nielsen report on television.* Northbrook, IL: A. C. Nielsen.

O'Keefe, G., & Reid-Nash, K. (1986). *The uses and effects of public service announcements.* Paper presented to the National Partnership to Prevent Alcohol and Drug Abuse, Washington, DC.

Osler, W. (1905). *Aequanimitas with other addresses: Internal medicine as a vocation.* Philadelphia: Blakistone.

Paisley, W. J. (1981). Public communication campaigns: The American experience. In R. E. Rice & W. J. Paisley (Eds.), *Public communication campaigns* (pp. 15-40). Beverly Hills, CA: Sage.

Palmer, E. (1981). Shaping persuasive messages with formative research. In R. E. Rice & W. J. Paisley (Eds.), *Public communication campaigns* (pp. 227-238). Beverly Hills, CA: Sage.

Pearce, M. R. (1979). The public arena of marketing. In C. J. Frey, T. C. Kinnear, & B. B. Reece (Eds.), *Public policy issues in marketing* (pp. 1-16). Ann Arbor: University of Michigan Press.

Pekurny, R. (1982). Coping with television production. In J. Ettema & D. C. Whitney (Eds.), *Individuals in mass media organizations: Creativity and constraint.* Beverly Hills, CA: Sage.

Peterkin, B. B. (1985). Dietary guidelines, 2nd edition. *Journal of Nutrition Education, 17*(5), 188-190.

Peterson, J. L., Moore, K. A., & Furstenberg, F. F. (in press). Television viewing and early initiation of sexual intercourse: Is there a link? *Journal of Homosexuality.*

Pierce, J., Dwyer, T., Frape, G., Chapman, S., Chamberlain, A., & Burke, N. (1986). Evaluation of the Sydney quit for life anti-smoking campaign. *Medical Journal of Australia, 144*, 341-347.

Population Reports. (1986). Radio spreading the word in family planning. J (32), 853-887.

Postman, N. (1985). *Amusing ourselves to death.* New York: Viking.

Prochaska, J. O., & DeClemente, C. C. (1983). Stages and processes of self-change of smoking: Toward an integrative model of change. *Journal of Consulting and Clinical Psychology, 51*, 390-395.

Puska, P., McAlister, A., & Maccoby, N. (1985). Planned use of mass media in national health promotion: The "keys to health" TV program in 1982 in Finland. *Canadian Journal of Public Health, 76*, 336-342.

Ray, M. L. (1973). Marketing communication and the hierarchy-of-effects. In P. Clarke (Ed.), *New models for mass communication research* (pp. 147-176). Beverly Hills, CA: Sage.

Reston, J. (1967). *Sketches in the sand.* New York: Alfred A. Knopf.

Roberts, D., & Bachen, C. (1978). *The impact of within-ad disclosures vs. supplemental nutrition messages on children's understanding of the concept of a balanced breakfast.* Technical report submitted to the Federal Trade Commission. Department of Communication, Stanford University.

Roberts, D., Gibson, W. A., & Bachen, C. (1979). *The impact of animated public service announcements on children's responses to questions about health and safety.* Technical report submitted to ABC Television, Inc.

Robertson, T. S., Rossiter, J. R., & Gleason, T. C. (1979). Children's receptivity to proprietary medicine advertising. *Journal of Consumer Research, 6*, 247-255.

Rogers, E. M., Aikat, S., Chang, S., Poppe, P., & Sopory, P. (1989). *Proceedings from the conference on entertainment-education for social change.* Los Angeles: Annenberg School of Communications, University of Southern California.

Rogers, E. M., & Shoemaker, F. F. (1971). *Communication of innovations.* New York: Free Press.

Rogers, E. M., & Singhal, A. (1989). Estrategías de educación entretenimiento. *Chasqui, 31*, 9-22.

Rogers, E. M., & Storey, J. D. (1987). Communication campaigns. In C. Berger & S. Chaffee (Eds.), *Handbook of communication science* (pp. 817-846). Newbury Park, CA: Sage.

Rossiter, J. R., & Robertson, T. S. (1980). Children's dispositions toward proprietary drugs and the role of television drug advertising. *Public Opinion Quarterly, 44*(3), 316-329.

Schorr, L. (1988). *Within our reach.* New York: Anchor/Doubleday.

Shaw, D. (1988, December 21). Hudson brought AIDS coverage out of the closet. *Los Angeles Times.*

Sherman, B. L., & Dominick, J. R. (1986). Violence and sex in music videos: TV and rock 'n' roll. *Journal of Communication, 36*(1), 79-93.

Signorielli, N. (1985). *Role portrayal and stereotyping on television: An annotated biliography of studies relating to women, minorities, aging, sexual behavior, health, and handicaps.* Westport, CT: Greenwood Press.

Signorielli, N. (1987). Drinking, sex, and violence on television: The cultural indicators perspective. *Journal of Drug Education, 17*(3), 245-260.

Singhal, A. (1990). *Entertainment-education communication strategies for development.* Unpublished doctoral dissertation, University of Southern California.

Singhal, A., & Rogers, E. (1989). Prosocial television for development in India. In R. E. Rice & C. K. Atkin (Eds.), *Public communication campaigns* (pp. 331-350). Newbury Park, CA: Sage.

Smith, F. A., Trivax, G., Zuehlke, D. A., Lowinger, P., & Nghiem, T. L. (1972). Health information during a week of television. *The New England Journal of Medicine, 286*(10), 516-520.

Smith, R. C. (1978, February). The magazines' smoking habit. *Columbia Journalism Review,* pp. 29-31.

Smoke signals. (1987). New York: American Cancer Society.

Smoking control media advocacy guidelines. (1988). Washington, DC: Advocacy Institute for the National Cancer Institute, National Institutes of Health.

Solomon, D. (1982). Health campaigns on television. In D. Pearl, L. Bouthilet, & J. Lazar (Eds.), *Television and behavior: Ten years of scientific progress and implications for the eighties* (pp. 308-321). Rockville, MD: National Institute of Mental Health.

Stanton, J. L. (1987, November 9). No rush to health claims. *Advertising Age,* p. 18.

Stone, C. (1988). *Second national survey on "Naseberry Street" programme.* Unpublished manuscript, University of West Indies, Mona.

Strouse, J., & Fabes, R. A. (1985). Formal vs. informal sources of sex education: Competing forces in the sexual socialization of adolescents. *Adolescence, 20,* 251-263.

Syme, L., & Berkman, L. (1981). Social class, susceptibility, and sickness. In P. Conrad & R. Kern (Eds.), *Sociology of health and illness* (pp. 35-44). New York: St. Martin's Press.

Taylor, E. (1987, August 16). TV dramas: Sweet agreement, little grit. *New York Times.*

Taylor, P. (1984). *The smoke ring.* New York: Pantheon.

Televisa's Institute for Communication Research (1981). *Toward the social use of soap operas.* Paper presented to International Institute of Communication, Strasbourg, France.

TIO/Roper (1989). *America's watching: The 1989 TIO/Roper report.* Washington, DC: National Association of Broadcasters.

Tucker, L. A. (1986). The relationship of television viewing to physical fitness and obesity. *Adolescence, 21,* 797-806.

Turow, J. (1982). Unconventional programs on commercial television: An organizational perspective. In J. Ettema & D. C. Whitney (Eds.), *Individuals in mass media organizations: Creativity and constraint.* Beverly Hills, CA: Sage.

Turow, J. (1984). *Media industries: The production of news and entertainment.* New York: Longman.

Turow, J. (1985). The influence of pressure groups on television entertainments. In W. Rowland & B. Watkins (Eds.), *Interpreting television* (pp. 142-162). Beverly Hills, CA: Sage.

Turow, J. (1989). *Playing doctor: Television, storytelling, and medical power.* New York: Oxford University Press.

Turow, J., & Coe, L. (1985). Curing television's ills: The portrayal of health care. *Journal of Communication, 35*(4), 36-51.

Wallack, L., Breed, W., & Cruz, J. (1987). Alcohol on primetime television. *Journal of Studies on Alcohol, 48*(1), 33-38.

Wallack, L., Breed, W., & De Foe, J. R. (1985). Alcohol and soap operas: Drinking in the light of day. *Journal of Drug Education, 15*(4), 365-379.

Wallack, L., Grube, T. W., Madden, P. A., & Breed, W. (in press). Portrayals of alcohol in prime-time television. *Journal of Studies in Alcohol.*

Warner, K. E. (1981). Cigarette smoking in the 1970's: The impact of the anti-smoking campaigns on consumption. *Science, 211,* 729-731.

Warner, K. E. (1985). Cigarette advertising and media coverage of smoking and health. *The New England Journal of Medicine, 312*(6), 384-388.

Warner, K. E. (1986). *Selling smoke: Cigarette advertising and public health.* Washington, DC: American Public Health Association.

Weis, W. L., & Burke, C. (1986). Media content and tobacco advertising: An unhealthy addiction. *Journal of Communication, 36*(4), 59-69.

Whalan, E. M., Sheridan, M. J., Meister, K. A., & Mosher, B. A. (1981). Analysis of coverage of tobacco hazards in women's magazines. *Journal of Public Health Policy, 2,* 28-35.

Whelan, E. M., & Stanko, R. T. (1983). Medically muddled media. *Journal of the American Medical Association, 250*(16), 2137.

White, L. C. (1988). *Merchants of death.* New York: Beech Tree/Morrow.

White, L., & Whelan, E. (1986). How well do American magazines cover the health hazards of smoking? *ACSH News and Views, 7*(3), 8-11.

Winnard, K., Rimon, J., & Convisser, J. (1987). *The impact of television on the family planning attitudes of an urban Nigerian audience.* Paper presented at the American Public Health Association.

Winsten, J. A. (1985). Science and the media: The boundaries of truth. *Health Affairs, 6.*

Worden, J. K., Flynn, B. S., Geller, B. M., Chen, M., Shelton, L. G., Secker-Walker, R. H., Solomon, D. S., Solomon, L. J., Couchey, S., & Constanza, M. C. (1989). *Development of a smoking prevention mass media program using diagnostic and formative research.* Unpublished manuscript.

Yankelovich, Skelly, and White, Inc. (1979). *The General Mills American family report 1978-79: Family health in an era of stress.* Minneapolis, MN: General Mills.

Zillmann, D., & Bryant, J. (1985). *Selective exposure to communication.* Hillsdale, NJ: Earlbaum.

Zillmann, D., & Bryant, J. (in press). Pornography's impact on sexual satisfaction. *Journal of Applied Psychology.*

Index

About the Authors

ELAINE BRATIC ARKIN is a consultant with 20 years of experience in developing and managing health communications programs for the public, patients, and health professionals. Her clients include national voluntary and governmental agencies concerned with communicating effectively about issues such as AIDS, drugs and alcohol, smoking, cancer, nutrition, and environmental risks.

CHARLES ATKIN (Ph.D., University of Wisconsin) is Professor in the Departments of Communication and Telecommunication at Michigan State University, where he investigates mass media effects. His current research focuses on health campaigns, particularly prevention of alcohol misuse and risky driving. He recently co-edited *Public Communication Campaigns* (Sage) with Ronald E. Rice.

DEE BURTON's research interests include all aspects of tobacco control, and the use of mass media for health promotion. Her current research focuses on tobacco cessation interventions for adolescents and older confirmed smokers, and cross-cultural differences in response to tobacco advertising. Dr. Burton is Associate Director for Media Research of the University of Illinois-Chicago Prevention Research

Center, and Assistant Professor in the Community Health Sciences Department of the UIC School of Public Health.

ROBERT DENNISTON is Director, Division of Communication Programs, Office for Substance Abuse Prevention of the U.S. Public Health Service. He has responsibility for various alcohol and other drug-related communications projects, including media programs, communications grants, training and technical assistance, and development of communications-related partnerships with public and private sector organizations.

GEORGE DESSART was Vice President, Programming Practices, CBS Broadcast Group, at the time he participated as an industry representative in the Rancho Mirage conference. He is currently with Dessart Communications Associates in Valley Cottage, New York.

BRIAN R. FLAY is Associate Professor and Director, Prevention Research Center, School of Public Health, University of Illinois-Chicago. He has conducted extensive research examining the role of mass media in smoking cessation and drug abuse prevention. His methodological specialty is the design of summative research for evaluating prevention campaigns.

STEPHEN KLAIDMAN is a Senior Research Fellow with the Kennedy Institute of Ethics and a research consultant with the Department of Community and Family Medicine, both of Georgetown University. He recently published *The Virtuous Journalist* (Oxford University Press) with Tom Beauchamp. He has served as an editor and writer for the *International Herald Tribune, The Washington Post*, and *The New York Times*.

PHILIP MEYER is William Rand Kenan Professor in the School of Journalism at University of North Carolina, following a 21-year career as a practicing journalist with the Knight-Ridder newspapers. He is the author of *Ethical Journalism* (Longman) and *Precision Journalism* (Indiana University Press).

KATHRYN C. MONTGOMERY is Assistant Professor of Film and Television at UCLA, specializing in broadcast history, telecommunications policy, media criticism, and public health issues in the media. She is the leading expert on advocacy groups and entertainment television, the subject of her recently published book, *Target: Prime Time* (Oxford University Press). Montgomery is also a TV critic and commentator for National Public Radio.

WILLIAM NOVELLI (M.B.A., University of Pennsylvania), is President of Porter, Novelli, and Associates in Washington, D.C. A specialist in social marketing and advertising, he has taught at the University of Maryland.

MICHAEL PERTSCHUK directs the Advocacy Institute in Washington, D.C., where he is developing media advocacy strategies focusing on smoking issues. He was Chairman of the Federal Trade Commission during the Carter administration

EVERETT M. ROGERS (Ph.D., Iowa State University) is Professor of Communications, Annenberg School of Communications, University of Southern California. His research interests include the diffusion of innovations, development communication, and social impact of new media technologies. Most recently, he has been studying the enter-education approach to media campaigning.

ROSE MARY ROMANO (MA, Community Health Education, New York University) is Chief, Public Information Branch, Office on Smoking and Health, Centers for Disease Control, where she directs an extensive media program targeted to teenagers, women, and minorities. She was formerly Chief of the Information Project Branch of the National Cancer Institute, and has served as adviser to many national health communication programs

NANCY SIGNORIELLI (Ph.D., University of Pennsylvania) was Research Administrator of the Cultural Indicators Project before taking her current position as Associate Professor at the University of Delaware. Her studies have focused on mass media imagery of women and minorities, and televison and children. Signorielli and Michael Morgan are co-editors of *Cultivation Analysis* (Sage).

BRUCE A. SILVERGLADE (J.D., Boston College) is Legal Affairs Director of the Center for Science in the Public Interest, a nonprofit consumer advocacy organization in Washington, D.C. He coordinates

CSPI's legislative activities on food and environmental health. He has also worked in the Federal Trade Commission's Bureau of Consumer Protection and Office of Policy and Planning.

ARVIND SINGHAL is completing his doctoral studies at the Annenberg School of Communications at the University of Southern California. He conducts research on development communication and the social impacts of new media technologies.

STEPHEN C. STUYCK is Associate Vice President for Public Affairs at the University of Texas M. D. Anderson Cancer Center in Houston, where he also serves as Assistant to the President. He is currently principal investigator for the M. D. Anderson's Cancer Information Service contract with the National Cancer Institute. He recently completed a year as regional chairman of the Group on Public Affairs of the Association of American Medical Colleges.

LAWRENCE WALLACK, Doctor of Public Health, is Associate Professor in the School of Public Health, University of California-Berkeley. He has published extensively on the prevention of public health problems, emphasizing the mass media's role and alcohol-related issues.

NOTES

NOTES